Raising a
Spiritually
Strong
Daughter

Raising a Spiritually Strong Daughter

GUIDING HER TOWARD A FAITH THAT LASTS

SUSIE SHELLENBERGER

BETHANYHOUSE

MINNEAPOLIS, MINNESOTA

Published by Bethany House Publishers
11400 Hampshire Avenue South
Bloomington, Minnesota 55438

Bethany House Publishers is a division of
Baker Publishing Group, Grand Rapids, Michigan.

Printed in the United States of America

In keeping with biblical principles of
creation stewardship, Baker Publishing Group advocates the responsible
use of our natural resources. As a
member of the Green Press Initiative,
our company uses recycled paper
when possible. The text paper of
this book is comprised of 30% post-
consumer waste.

green
press
INITIATIVE

Library of Congress Cataloging-in-Publication Data

Shellenberger, Susie.
   Raising a spiritually strong daughter : guiding her toward a faith that lasts / Susie
Shellenberger.
     p. cm.
   Summary: "Advice for a Christian mom wishing to instill her God-honoring values in
her daughter and to foster the development of her daughter's relationship with Christ"—
Provided by publisher.
   ISBN 978-0-7642-0376-3 (pbk. : alk. paper) 1. Mothers and daughters—Religious
aspects—Christianity. 2. Daughters—Religious life. 3. Teenage girls—Religious life.
I. Title.
   BV4529.18.S5326   2009
   248.8'45—dc22
                                        2009014975

To my spiritual heritage—those who have and who continue to speak God's truth into my life. They are . . .

My parents, Elmer and Marjorie Shellenberger,
Thank you for giving me such a strong spiritual heritage!

Mother, your no-compromise faith in Christ still inspires me. Now that you're with God personally, I'm wondering if He's telling you all the stuff I'm asking Him to pass on to you, or if He's waiting to let me do it in person when I join you in heaven. At any rate, I can't wait to spend eternity with you, and I'm excited to catch you up on all He's doing in my life since you entered heaven.

Dad, I'll never forget the Sunday afternoon Bible stories from that big red book you shared with me just before you dozed off on your weekly nap. Your rendering of Daniel, the three Hebrew children, Job, and all the others weren't simply stories. You shared them in such a way that made me believe in their truth; they were reality; they could be my story if I trusted God. And they have inspired me to trust the same God they did and to absorb the Bible as absolute truth. I long to meet my Bible heroes and see if their faces match our imagination.

Lawana, my new mother, thank you for praying for me daily. Do you know how much strength that gives me? I see Jesus in your cheerfulness, your smile, and your positive attitude. I strive to imitate your qualities—that in turn reflect Christ—in my own life.

SUSIE SHELLENBERGER was founding editor of Focus on the Family's *Brio* magazine for teen girls in 1990 and continued to serve as editor for nearly two decades. A former youth pastor and high school teacher, Susie has written more than forty books, is in demand as an international speaker for women's groups and teens, and started the *Brio* Mother-Daughter Cruise for Focus on the Family. Susie lives in Colorado Springs and recently launched *Susie*, a new magazine for teen girls.

CONTENTS

JOB OPENING

POSITION: Mother, Mom, Mama, Mommy

Job Description: Long-term team player needed for challenging work in an often chaotic environment. Candidate must be willing to work variable hours, including evenings, weekends, and frequent twenty-four-hour shifts. Some overnight travel required, including trips to primitive camping sites on rainy weekends and endless sports tournaments in faraway cities. Travel expenses not reimbursed.

Skills Required: The candidate must be willing to be hated—at least temporarily—until someone needs five dollars. Must be willing to bite tongue repeatedly. Must be willing to be indispensable one minute and an embarrassment the next. Must handle assembly and product safety testing of half a million cheap plastic toys and battery-operated devices. Ability to treat flesh wounds a plus. Must be able to think outside the box but not lose track of the box, because you most likely will need it for a school project.

Other Responsibilities: Must be proficient in managing resources fairly unless you want to hear "He got more than me" for the rest of your life. Candidate must be able to drive motor vehicles safely under loud and adverse conditions while simultaneously practicing skills in conflict resolution.

Possibility for Advancement and Promotion: Virtually none. Your job is to remain in the same position for years, without complaining, while constantly retraining and updating your skills so that those in your charge can ultimately surpass you.

Wages and Compensation: You pay them! A balloon payment is due when the offspring turn eighteen because of the assumption that college will help them become financially independent. When you die, you give them whatever is left. The oddest thing about this reverse-salary scheme is that you actually enjoy it and wish you could do more.

Benefits: While there is no health insurance, no pension, and no paid holidays, this job supplies limitless opportunities for personal growth and free hugs for life.

Chapter 1

PLAYING COPYCAT

Mom, the most important job you'll ever have has nothing to do with your career, your position, or your title in the workplace. Your most important job of all time—and the highest call on your life—is to guide your children into an eternal relationship with Jesus Christ.

Because this book is specifically geared toward moms of girls, we'll focus solely on your daughter. But many of these principles will relate to sons as well. And though I'll most often refer to your daughter in the singular, I realize many reading this will have more than one daughter. Please keep in mind that an approach that works with one daughter may not be the best approach for another daughter. Oftentimes you'll simply learn by doing, trying, and trying again.

Being a mom is a full-time job. Even if you're employed outside the home, you've probably realized that motherhood is still a full-time position.

I'm not aware of any other job besides motherhood that requires such specific and so many varied responsibilities. You probably read the job description for motherhood on the opposite page. And you know, as extensive and humorous as that was, it still wasn't exhaustive. We could also add the following:

- Ability to discern when discipline is needed and how much and what kind is most appropriate at the time
- Ability to dispense grace, hugs, and affirmation consistently
- Enough medical knowledge to medicate and care for a variety of illnesses, broken bones, and broken hearts
- Counseling skills
- Sufficient education to help with spelling, arithmetic, English, history, algebra, geography, and at least one foreign language
- Veterinary skills to care for the hamsters, snakes, cats, dogs, and other animals your daughter brings home
- Security training to provide a sense of protection for school, friends, dates, and part-time jobs
- Occupational therapist skills to assess functional needs and to help develop potential life skills

As a mom, *you* are your daughter's greatest influence! Can you say with confidence as the apostle Paul did in 1 Corinthians 4:16, "Therefore I urge you to imitate me"?

Determine right now to be such a reflection of Christ that you *can* say with confidence, "Imitate me."

Does this mean you're to be perfect? Well, Jesus does tell us in Matthew 5:48, "Be perfect, therefore, as your heavenly Father is perfect." But before you toss this book on the floor thinking, *I'm giving up; that's impossible*, stick with me for some good news.

PERFECT = COMPLETE

We tend to equate *perfect* with *behavior*, don't we? *I need to bite my tongue more. I shouldn't have reacted that way. Why did I say that? Why am I so angry?*

But if we were to grab a Greek dictionary and some Bible commentaries, we'd discover that in this context, the Greek word *perfect* isn't determined by behavior. Christ isn't telling us that we have to be perfect humans—that's impossible. He's using the word *perfect* to describe being whole with our heavenly Father. God wants to perfect your heart. He wants to make you complete. He wants your wholeness to be found in Him.

And that's good news!

Why?

Because once you've allowed God to perfect your heart, the Holy Spirit will begin the transformation process of making you like Him. You've already been made in His image (Genesis 1:26), but you won't begin reflecting His likeness until you've totally submitted to the power of His Holy Spirit.

And once you do? His likeness begins to develop in your life through specific characteristics: love, joy, peace, patience, kindness, goodness, faithfulness, gentleness, and self-control (Galatians 5:22–23). Sound familiar? Those qualities are actually the fruit of His Holy Spirit.

WHO WILL BE THE GREATEST INFLUENCE?

It's an obvious fact: Your teen daughter is being influenced every day of her life. So take charge! Decide that *you* will be her greatest influence.

But that scares me, you may be thinking. *And if I can get past the fear factor, how do I become her greatest influence?* You will get past the fear factor—if you'll stick with me until the end of this book—and you can become her greatest influence by pointing her to the One who will influence her not only now but throughout eternity. That's what this book is about. We'll journey together—two friends conversationally navigating this important process—on how you can give your daughter faith everlasting!

LET'S PRAY

Because I don't know where you're coming from, can we take a few minutes to pray together? If you don't know Jesus Christ as your personal Savior—if you've never confessed your sins and accepted His forgiveness, if you don't truly have a genuine *relationship* with Him—you're not actually a Christian. The Bible is clear that we don't simply inherit Christ. We must accept His free gift of salvation, and that requires action on our part. Yes, the gift is free. But to receive it is action oriented. It requires belief and faith.

If you're not a Christian, you won't be able to raise your daughter with a solid faith in Christ. If you'd like to make the decision to ask Christ into your life and commit yourself to following Him, I invite you to turn to page 223 and pray the prayer of salvation. Then meet me back here. (If you're already a Christian, living in a genuine, growing relationship with Christ, keep reading.)

"IMITATE ME"

Being able to say "Imitate me" to your daughter is essentially saying that your lifestyle so clearly reflects Christ's, you're encouraging your daughter to be your copycat. *How is that possible?* you may be thinking.

It's possible by becoming complete in Christ. Remember the Scripture from Matthew 5:48: "Be perfect, therefore, as your heavenly Father is perfect."

Again, God doesn't expect you to be perfect in your humanness, but He does want to perfect your heart! And with a perfect heart—in being whole and complete in Christ—you can confidently tell your daughter to imitate your lifestyle.

Let's break it down even further.

You may already be a Christian. If so, then you've asked Christ to forgive your sins, and He has! "[We] are justified freely by his grace through the redemption that came by Christ Jesus" (Romans 3:24).

As a Christian, you have the assurance your sins are forgiven. But may I challenge you on a deeper level?

Okay, here goes!

Though your sins are forgiven, your sinful nature is still inside you.

God wants to completely cleanse you of your sinful nature!

This is done through sanctification by the Holy Spirit. Having your sins forgiven but still living with a sinful nature won't allow you to live a holy life.

Why is that important? you may be asking.

It's important because God demands our holiness.

Yes . . . when I get to heaven I can live a holy life, but not here on earth!

It's possible to live a holy life on earth, or God wouldn't have demanded it. Think about it: You serve a God of possibility, a God of miracles, a God of reality! He doesn't treat you like a dog—holding a piece of meat in front of you, saying, "Come on! Work for it! Jump!"

He's not a God of frustration. He's a God of fulfillment. He doesn't say "Be holy, because I am holy" (1 Peter 1:16; Leviticus 11:44) to frustrate you with something that's impossible.

The same God who says "Be holy, because I am holy" gives you everything you need to make that command a reality. The equipment? The tool? His very Spirit saturating and energizing your life!

How can His Spirit make me holy? you may ask.

Through total surrender on your part, God will release the power of His Spirit throughout your life.

I thought I already had the Holy Spirit.

You do. When you became a Christian, you received all of God: the Father, the Son, and the Holy Spirit. But it could be that God didn't receive all of you. Though the Holy Spirit is living inside you, you won't truly begin to live inside His power until you've completely surrendered your life to make Christ absolute Lord.

YOU'RE NOT ALONE

Paul experienced this struggle. In Romans 7:15–25, he describes his frustration in being a Christian still enslaved to sin. He says that he wants to do what pleases God, but he finds himself still doing the things that break God's heart. He tells us that he made a conscious decision in his mind to follow Christ (just like many of us have), but sin still has a grip on him.

For ten verses, Paul goes in circles describing his journey of frustration. Maybe you've experienced it too: You know what's right and what will please God, but you end up doing the wrong thing.

Finally, in chapter eight, Paul discovers the answer. He tells us there is freedom from sin through the sanctifying power of the Holy Spirit.

Let's imagine someone just like us, and use her to explain what happens.

MEET SARAH

When Sarah became a Christian, she asked Christ to forgive her sins, and He did! She committed her life to Him and began a relationship with Jesus.

But at some point in her Christian life—the longer she walks with Him—she begins to realize an important truth: God demands holiness.

She begins thinking, *I try and try to be holy, to do what's right, to stay away from the same old sin* (jealousy, gossip, sexually explicit TV shows and movies, bitterness, drunkenness, etc.), *but I usually end up going back and doing things I know are displeasing to God. I just can't be holy. I don't have enough power. I mean, for me to really live a holy life, would require some kind of supernatural power!*

Good news!

God has that supernatural power! And He wants to release it into every area of Sarah's life through His Holy Spirit.

When she comes to that point of realization, she doesn't have to start all over again. "Okay, maybe this third time I become a Christian, I'll get it right." No. She's already a Christian, remember?

She can start right where she is! She thanks God that He has forgiven her sins, but she admits to Him that the sinful nature is still inside her heart, drawing her to do things displeasing to Him. So Sarah asks Him to remove the sinful nature from her life and to release the power of His Holy Spirit that's within her.

Wait a minute! you're probably thinking. *How is it possible to live a human life without a sinful nature?*

It's not only possible but realistic to live a human life—through the power of the Holy Spirit—without a sinful nature. It's not possible, however, to live without a human nature. There's a difference.

When you totally surrender everything to Christ—when you decide to live in radical obedience to His lordship—He perfects your heart. No, your human actions don't become perfect (remember, perfection in this case doesn't equal behavior), but you truly become complete in Him. And a perfect heart doesn't want to displease God. (It's a matter of allowing God to change your "want to." Your "want"—your greatest desire—is now to please Him. You don't want to sin anymore.)

COMPLETE IN HIM

The deepest desire of a perfect heart in Christ is to do His will. Your heart cry becomes, "Jesus, I want to duplicate you in front of my family and friends. I don't want to offer my own opinions, judgments, or actions until I first weigh them against yours. And if my opinions, judgments, and actions don't pass, then I don't offer them, or I change them to reflect yours."

God begins to transform your opinions, judgments, and actions to His own! "Do not conform any longer to the pattern of this world, but be transformed by the renewing of your mind. Then you will be able to test and approve what God's will is—his good, pleasing and perfect will" (Romans 12:2).

When our friend Sarah gives everything to God, and when God releases the power of His very Spirit within her, she begins to live a holy life. Does that mean she's perfect in behavior? No, she's still human. God won't transform her humanity until she's in heaven. But she's living with a perfect *heart*; she's living in completion and in wholeness with her heavenly Father.

Will Sarah still sin?

To answer that, we first have to define sin. I define sin as *a willful act of disobedience against the known will of God.* Using that definition, consider this: If Sarah knows that God wants her to stop corresponding with a man in a chat room, and she continues anyway, has she sinned? Yes.

If God tells her to share His plan of salvation with someone in a chat room, and she doesn't do it, has she sinned? Yes.

If she's battling a migraine and is a little short with a co-worker, has she sinned? No. That's something she needs to work on, and she may need to apologize, but she hasn't deliberately set out to disobey her heavenly Father.

Sin is when we willfully and consciously decide to go against God's will.

Now that Sarah is sanctified wholly, will she still sin?

She doesn't have to.

What?!

Remember our definition of sin: deliberately and willfully going against God's will.

With the Holy Spirit's power saturating and guiding every area of her life—and with Sarah's heart cry truly desiring to do God's will—when she's tempted to sin, she *can* say no. She no longer has to rely on her own human strength to say no. She now has a supernatural power within her that she can rely on.

Listen to what the apostle John says: "My dear children, I write this to you so that you will not sin" (1 John 2:1). John—the disciple closest to Christ during His time on earth—wouldn't have said that if it weren't possible!

When Sarah is tempted, she *can* choose to rely on the Holy Spirit's power saturating her lifestyle and say, "No! I recognize this temptation is leading me to go against God's will. In His mighty power within me, I'm saying NO to this temptation, and I'm turning away from it."

Sarah doesn't have to sin.

But . . . read what John has to say in the very next sentence: "But if anybody does sin, we have one who speaks to the Father in our defense—Jesus Christ, the Righteous One" (1 John 2:1).

By relying on the power of the Holy Spirit within her, Sarah doesn't *have* to sin, but she's still human . . . and she still *might* sin.

If she does, she doesn't have to become a Christian all over again; she's already a Christian. If she sins, the Holy Spirit, who's now guiding every area of her life, will convict her. He'll let her know that she disobeyed the Father. And when He makes this clear to her, Sarah repents of the sin and accepts His forgiveness and continues her relationship with Him. That's spiritual growth. That's living a holy life.

TOUGH STUFF

God has extremely strong things to say to Christians who deliberately and willfully continue to live in sin:

> Not everyone who says to me, "Lord, Lord" will enter the kingdom of heaven, but only he who does the will of my Father who is in heaven.
>
> Matthew 7:21

> Don't fool yourselves! Those who live immoral lives, who are idol worshipers, adulterers or homosexuals—will have no share in His Kingdom. Neither will thieves or greedy people, drunkards, slanderers or robbers.
>
> 1 Corinthians 6:9 TLB

Guess who the apostle was writing to in the above verse? People who called themselves Christians!

> Someone may say, "I am a Christian; I am on my way to heaven; I belong to Christ." But if he doesn't do what Christ tells him to, he is a liar.
>
> 1 John 2:4 TLB

John is talking about Christians who willfully and deliberately continue to live in disobedience to God.

> But those who do what Christ tells them to will learn to love God more and more. That is the way to know whether or not you are a Christian. Anyone who says he is a Christian should live as Christ did.
>
> 1 John 2:5–6 TLB

RECAP

Why is it a big deal that you become sanctified?

1. Because God commands it. It's God's will that you should be sanctified. (See 1 Thessalonians 4:3.)

2. Because unless you *are* sanctified, you won't be able to say to your daughter, "Imitate me as I imitate Christ." You need His supernatural power to live that out!

3. If you're *not* sanctified, you won't be able to lead your daughter into a sanctified life.

Have you totally surrendered to the authority of the Holy Spirit's leading in your life?

If you'd like to become a mom of spiritual influence—a mom who exhibits the fruit of God's Spirit—and a mom who can confidently say, "Imitate me," I encourage you to pray this prayer with me:

Dear Jesus,

Thank you for forgiving my sins and helping me establish a genuine relationship with you. But I want more; I *need* more. My daughter is watching me. I want to be able to say, as the apostle Paul did to his followers, "Imitate me."

I want to live so close to you—to be so intimately connected with you—that by imitating my life, my daughter will actually be imitating you.

It's obvious I can't do this on my own. That's why I'm coming to you now. I'm already a Christian, and you've forgiven my sins, but sin is still in my life. I'm still living with a carnal nature. I don't want that.

Will you remove the sinful nature from me and release the power of your Holy Spirit to saturate every part of my entire life? I surrender everything I've been, everything I am, and everything I'll become to you right now.

Jesus, I not only give you my life, I give you my rights as well. I give you my very *self.* I'm dying to *me* right now, and I'm asking you to live through my body instead of me. Use me to bring glory to your name.

Will you perfect my heart and make me complete in you? I want to be whole in you, Jesus. I want you to transform me into your image. I want my deepest desire to be to please you, to do your will.

I realize that I don't have to yield to temptation. Through your supernatural power now saturating every area of my life, I *can* lean on you and say no to sin.

But I'm still human, Jesus. You know that, because you created me. I don't ever want to sin again. I don't ever want to deliberately go against your holy will. But if I do, please prick my heart with your Holy Spirit to help me know that I've done wrong. And when you do that—when you bring it to my attention—I'll admit my sin and will seek your forgiveness. Then I'll continue to follow you.

Dear Jesus, I really want to be *you* to my daughter. I want to be the greatest influence in her life, and I want to consistently shine to reflect you.

You're in charge, Jesus.

I give my daughter to you.

And I'm trusting you to show me how to be *you* to her.

Thank you for making me complete in you, and for releasing the power of your Spirit throughout every area of my life.

I love you, Jesus.

I pray these things in your holy name.

Amen.

NOW WHAT?

If you prayed that prayer, you need to realize that God's mighty power truly is within you. Wow! That's a lot of power! Think about it: The same mighty power that hung the stars in the sky and set the whole world in motion is now within *you*.

The same mighty power that made blind people see, deaf folks hear, and lame men walk is now guiding your life.

That's a lot of power!

What will you do with it? You'll live your life in it!

Don't let it become dormant—just sitting inside you. Live your life every single day in His holy power.

How do I do that? you may ask.

Here is an easy two-step strategy:

1. Pray every day. Don't simply talk to God about yourself and your daughter; tell Him everything!
2. Read your Bible every day. Even if it's only one minute a day, make time to read the Bible. You don't have to spend half an hour in God's Word for Him to act. If you spend only a minute a day absorbing truth through Scripture, you'll still be amazed at God's power working through your actions and reactions.

And if I skip a day? Don't beat yourself up! You're not going to hell if you don't read the Bible and pray every day. But if you *will* read the Bible and pray every day, you'll truly be living in His supernatural power. And that will enable you to say to your daughter, "Honey, watch my life and imitate me."

ONE MORE THING

Now that you've made the surrendering commitment to be sanctified, God will *continue* to transform you into His likeness. In other words, your commitment was a singular action, but the adventure of becoming like Him is a process. And turning everything over to God doesn't guarantee that you won't pick it up again. But when you do, the Holy Spirit will nudge you: "You gave that to me, remember? Let me help you release it once again." Again, your walk with Him is a process.

The goal of this book is to guide you into raising spiritually strong daughters. A girl looks to her mom for guidance, affirmation, and cues about life. As your daughter looks to you, she'll actually be seeing Christ through you. And that's the absolute essential in raising a spiritually strong daughter!

Chapter 2

YOUR DAUGHTER'S MOST IMPORTANT RELATIONSHIP

Though your relationship with your daughter is extremely special, her bond with you really isn't her most important relationship. The most important relationship she'll ever have—the one that will not only take her through life but take her through eternity—is her relationship with her Creator.

If your daughter is already a Christian, you may not feel the need to read this chapter. I'd like you to read it anyway, or at least skim it. It could help you guide another mom whose daughter isn't a Christian.

IS YOUR DAUGHTER A CHRISTIAN?

Do you know—really know—if your daughter has a genuine relationship with Christ? Yes, she may attend church with you. Yes, she may be involved in youth group and Bible study. Yes, she may hang out with Christian friends, love praise and worship, and even desire to participate in a missions trip. But do you know beyond all doubt that she really has a *relationship* with Christ?

I lead a two-week international missions trip every summer for teen guys and girls. Part of the application process requires them to define what a Christian is, talk about their involvement in their church, and have a pastor's recommendation. We take between six hundred and eight hundred people on this trip each summer. With this kind of application, you'd assume everyone we take is a Christian. I mean, they're testifying to that fact by the way they complete the application!

But you'd be surprised. Each summer a handful of students approach me toward the end of the trip saying, "I really thought I was a Christian when I applied for this trip. But after experiencing everything I have in the past two weeks, and after hearing your evening messages, I realized I really wasn't a Christian. But I am now!"

Because of that, we changed the layout of our program. We all convene in Miami for three days of intensive training before flying out to the country where we'll minister. When we began the trips, we started the first evening with cultural training and casting the vision for reaching the lost. We've now moved that to day two, and on the very first night, we have an evening we call Big Birtha. "Birtha" is short for *birthday*, and we call it this because we want students to know that their biggest and most important "birtha"—or birthday—is their spiritual one.

It's a simple evangelistic message that explains what being a Christian is. We talk about the necessity of confessing one's sins to Christ, having a repentant heart, seeking His forgiveness and placing our trust in Him to forgive us, and thanking Him for giving us new life. We encourage anyone who hasn't actually done that to do so.

We explain that we're in no shape to travel to another country and lead others to Christ if we as individuals don't have a personal relationship with Him. Every single year, on that very first night, we have students who pray the sinner's prayer and place their trust in

Christ. These are students who thought they were Christians; after all, they're good kids, they go to church, they're on a missions trip. But they're students who had never actually asked Christ to come into their hearts and forgive their sins.

SEARCHING FOR TEN YEARS

One of our adults arrived in Miami for leader training—which happens two days before the students arrive—and was eager to jump in and learn the ropes. But the next morning, her roommates cornered me and expressed their concern.

"Susie, we don't think Misty (not her real name) is a Christian."

"What you do mean?" I asked, knowing we had her testimony and her pastor's recommendation on her application, and that she wouldn't have been accepted if she had indicated she wasn't a Christian.

"Well, she has some very different ideas about God, and she's not married to the man she's living with."

Okay, those were major red flags to me!

So I cornered Misty a little later and began a conversation. "Misty, what brought you on this trip?"

"I heard you on a radio broadcast talking about the missions trip and all the miracles that happen, and I wanted to experience it."

I nodded my head in agreement, knowing lots of exciting things happen each summer on our trips. "Misty, tell me about your relationship with the Lord."

"Well, I've known God for a long time," she said. "And just the short time I've been here for leader training, I've grown so much. Susie, I'm learning a ton from your messages."

"Misty, tell me a little more about your relationship with the Lord. Can you tell me when you became a Christian?"

"Well, like I said, I've known God for years."

And then it hit me: Was she talking about God, the Father of Jesus Christ? Or was she talking about a "general" god that lots of people claim they know? So I pressed a little further. "Misty, a lot of people say they know God. And God can seem so general. But there's only one true God, and He's the Father of Jesus Christ. Do you have a relationship with Jesus?"

"No," she said. "I don't." Her answer was sure and to the point. "But I know God."

"Misty, I'm going to be a little blunt. Here's the truth: If you don't know His Son, Jesus, you don't really know God, the Father."

Sadly, she explained that she longed to know Jesus, but she knew she didn't have a relationship with Him. "Susie, I've searched for Jesus for ten years. I can't find Him. I can't seem to get a relationship with Him. But when I heard you on the radio, I thought if I came on this missions trip, maybe I could figure out how to find Jesus. And after I returned home it would possibly all fall together for me."

"Misty, it won't magically all fall together. Beginning a relationship with Christ is a conscious effort; it takes action. God will use His Holy Spirit to draw you to Him, and your response is to seek forgiveness for your sins and accept Christ as your personal Savior."

"I want to know Jesus."

I began to wonder if God had brought Misty on this trip not to be a leader to our teens, but so she could actually find Christ herself.

I knew she wasn't married, because her roommates had told me, but I needed to hear it from her. "Misty, are you married?"

"Well, no. But I know I'm with the man God wants me to be with. We just haven't gotten around to getting married yet."

"Misty, I'm going to be blunt with you again: You're living in sin. God is very clear about sexual relations outside of marriage. And for you to live with a man with whom you're not married is sin. That's standing in the way of your relationship with Christ."

I waited a few seconds for that to sink in, and then I continued.

"Misty, I challenge you to give your heart to Christ and begin a relationship with Him. And I also challenge you to call this man before we leave Miami and tell him to have either your bags packed or his bags packed by the time you get home, because you can't continue living together until you're married. I also want to take you out of a leadership role and just pour into your life for two weeks. Will you let us do that with you? Will you let us disciple you and just love on you and share Jesus with you for these next two weeks?"

She smiled from ear to ear. "You would do that for me?"

"Yes. I want you to be a helper, but not a leader. You need to grow in your faith and develop a relationship with Christ. Just let the rest of our leaders pour into your life, and you determine to help in any way you can, but don't allow yourself to lead students. Don't advise them, don't counsel them. Just love them."

She seemed happy with that option. I asked if I could pray with her and lead her into a relationship with Christ. She repeated a prayer after me, and I was excited with all the potential I could see in her.

A few hours later, Misty stopped me in the hall of our hotel. "Susie, after we prayed, I went up to my hotel room and knelt by my bed and began talking with the Lord. I told Him how sorry I was for my sins, and I clearly heard Him talking back to me!"

"That's great, Misty!" I said. "What did He say to you?"

"He told me that I'd spent years searching for Him, and all the while He was right here. The thing that kept me from truly having a relationship with Him was the fact that I wasn't willing to surrender. He asked me if I would surrender the man I'm living with and do things God's way. So I gave everything to Him, and I just got off the phone and told my man we can't live together until we're married. My next call is to our pastor to set a wedding date."

I rejoiced with Misty and excitedly watched her help in a variety of ways during the next two weeks. God is faithful, and God is patient, but He demands total surrender.

DIFFERENT GIRLS, DIFFERENT AGES

There's no magic age for when your daughter could become a Christian. She may be ready to accept Christ at age four, eight, or twelve. As soon as she can understand that she was born with sin and that Jesus loves her so much He died to pay for her sin, rose from the grave, and wants to have a relationship with her, she's ready to ask for forgiveness for her sins and to invite Christ into her life.

My friend Elizabeth has two daughters, Mia and Kaley. Mia is now in college, and Kaley is in high school. "Mia was an easy kid," Elizabeth says. "She didn't cry much as a baby, she slept through most of the night, and even as a child she was compliant and obedient."

But Kaley? You guessed it! Exactly the opposite. "While sweet-tempered Mia would do whatever I told her to, Kaley *always* bucked my authority."

And it was really more than that. Kaley was prone to throwing extreme tantrums. "It was awful," Elizabeth says. "Her eyes were filled with hate, and she'd scream and punch. It was completely out of hand. My husband and I prayed constantly for her."

Elizabeth's husband is a pastor, and he asked for others to help them pray that Kaley would allow God to change her life at a young age. They couldn't imagine heading into the school years with her monster behavior.

"No matter how much we disciplined her, it didn't help," Elizabeth says. "She simply became more angry and uncontrollable."

Elizabeth, her husband, and friends from church prayed hard for Kaley. "It finally happened," Elizabeth says. "One night when I was tucking her into bed, she began talking about the Sunday school lesson she'd heard earlier in the week. She was only four years old, but she said her Sunday school teacher told her that Jesus wanted us to be kind to each other."

Kaley's eyes filled with tears as Elizabeth held her daughter. "Mommy, I need Jesus to help me. I'm not nice."

Elizabeth wanted to turn somersaults and scream for her husband, but she remained calm and continued the conversation with her four-year-old daughter.

"Can Jesus help me, Mommy?"

"Yes, Kaley. He can. And He wants to!"

"I'm mean, Mommy. But I want to be nice."

Elizabeth led her daughter in a prayer that Kaley could understand. Kaley told the Lord she was sorry for being so mean, and she asked Him to forgive her of her sins. She told Jesus she loved Him and wanted His help to be nice to others.

"It was amazing," Elizabeth says. "She was a different person. It was night and day. Our prayers were answered for our little girl before she started elementary school."

Of course, Kaley's not perfect, but she's an amazing young lady who excels in track. She has become a people person. When I'm around her, I can't help but notice the magnetic way people are drawn to her. She's in love with Christ and still growing closer to Him.

Your daughter may not accept Christ when she's four; it may not be until she's twelve, a teenager, or even an adult. But saturate her life with prayer! God can and will make a difference.

BACK TO YOUR DAUGHTER

The most important question you'll ever ask your daughter is, "Do you have a personal relationship with Jesus Christ?"

I hope this doesn't scare you. I hope this isn't a tough question to ask. My dream for you is that you and your daughter are consistently talking about spiritual things and that this is an easy question to discuss together.

But if it *is* a tough question to ask, please don't be discouraged! You're on the right track! You're reading a book that will help guide you in helping your daughter establish a genuine faith in Christ.

Plan a special date with your daughter. It can be anything from a day of pampering (nails, free applications at the makeup counter, some time in a hot tub) to hiking and roasting hot dogs or reservations at a fancy restaurant. (You'll want to bring your Bible to this special event.) And during this special time, share with her how important your relationship with Christ is. Make sure she knows that it's the most important relationship you have and that it's eternal.

Explain the difference between knowing *about* Christ and knowing Him personally. Discuss what it means to have a relationship with Him. Talk about the components that make up a good earthly relationship, and transition to the fact that some of those same components are essential in a relationship with Christ. (Consistent communication, love, respect, admiration, a desire to grow closer.)

Tell your daughter how much you love her. Make sure she knows beyond doubt how important she is to you. Next, tell her how much you're looking forward to spending forever with her—in heaven. Then ask her if she has actually confessed her sins, sought forgiveness from Christ, placed her faith in Him, and established a genuine relationship with her Father.

If she has, ask her to talk about it. (Even if you already know the answers, it's good to go over this information.)

- "When did you ask Christ into your heart?"
- "Where were you?"
- "What were the surrounding circumstances?" (Was it at a Christian concert, at church camp, in her bedroom, at church?)

(If she hasn't asked Christ into her life, we'll get to that in a moment.)

Now it's your turn. Describe to your daughter what your life was like before you had a relationship with Christ. After you've shared with her, ask her if she has any questions for you. Be willing to discuss and answer those questions.

Now share with her the difference Christ has made in your life since you've placed your faith in Him. Again, ask her if she has any questions, and be willing to discuss and answer them.

Back to her. Now ask her to share what her life was like before she became a Christian. If she has trouble with this, you can help her with characteristics or attitudes she may have struggled with in the past (selfishness, the need to be first, disrespect, etc.).

Now ask her to think about the difference she sees in herself after allowing Christ to take control. End this special day by praying for each other. Make it a point from this day on to pray together consistently.

LEADING YOUR DAUGHTER TO CHRIST

If your daughter isn't a Christian, use this special time with her to explain that anyone who doesn't have a relationship with Him will be forever separated from God for all eternity. Again, explain how much you love her and want to spend forever with her in heaven.

Discuss the fact that we were all born with sin, and someone has to pay for that sin. It's either her . . . or Christ.

Either she'll die in sin, or she'll accept Christ's death as His special gift to her for payment of her sin and will live in heaven with Him for eternity.

Open your Bible and take turns reading these important Scriptures and discuss them together:

- We've all sinned and need a Savior. (Romans 3:23)
- God loves us so much, He wants to *give* us eternal life and forgive our sins as a *gift!* (Romans 6:23)
- How much does God love us? So much that He gave His one and only Son to pay the death penalty for *our* sins. (John

3:16)

- Jesus, God's Son, *willingly* gave His life for each one of us. (1 Peter 2:24)
- If we place our trust in Him, we can have forgiveness for our sins, and eternal life. (John 5:24)

Ask if she'd like to give her life to Christ and seek forgiveness for her sins. If she would, offer to pray this prayer with her and let her repeat it after you:

Dear Jesus,

I'm a sinner. I realize that I was born with sin, and the penalty is death. Thank you for loving me so much that you were willing to die in my place. Wow. That's a lot of love! I don't deserve that love, but I'm really grateful for it. Thanks for loving me that much!

I'm so sorry I've been sinning. I've been doing my own thing and have had bad attitudes and have disappointed you. Will you forgive me for all my sins? I believe you died on the cross for me. And I also believe that you rose from the dead and are alive right now. I know someday you're coming back to rescue all those who belong to you, so I want to be in your family.

Dear Jesus, I want to live forever in heaven with you. Right now I'm placing my trust in you. I accept your forgiveness for my sins. I accept your free gift of salvation. I want to live for you now. I want to glorify you in all I do and say.

Please help me to get to know you better. Help me to allow you to change my life to reflect your love to everyone I come in contact with.

I love you, Jesus.

And I thank you from the bottom of my heart for saving me from my sins.

I pray this in your holy name.

Amen.

AFTER YOUR DAUGHTER HAS ACCEPTED CHRIST

You'll want to talk with your pastor about baptism—a wonderful testimony to others of what God has done in your daughter's life. Baptism is two things: a testimony, and an act of obedience. Jesus himself was baptized, and He told His followers to be baptized as well. So please pray about this wonderful part of your daughter's spiritual journey. If you've never been baptized, it would be an incredibly special moment for the two of you to be baptized in the same service.

"Only Clark Kent had to be Superman,
but every mother has to be Superwoman."

—Ellen Bravo, former director of 9to5, the
National Association of Working Women

Chapter 3

READY, SET, GROW!

One of the best gifts you can give your daughter or daughters is to start pouring into her life at an early age. Your job to disciple her doesn't begin when she turns twelve or gets her driver's license. It begins at birth.

Huh? How can I disciple a baby?

You can provide Christian lullabies for her to listen to. You can even pray over her while she's still in the womb. And for a toddler, you can provide fun and captivating DVDs that tell Christian stories. (I can't help but think of VeggieTales right now. They're a great way to introduce children to Bible stories.)

And as your daughters grow, find age-appropriate devotional books for them to read on their own or for you to read with them. I'll never forget the first devotional book I read on my own. I was in grade school and at a district assembly for our church denomination (where several churches would gather together for special services). I discovered a devotional book written just for children, titled *Devotions With Julie and Jack*.

Long out of print (it can't even be found on *Amazon.com*!), it began each day with a fictional scenario of a brother-sister duo named Jack and Julie. Each day I learned a biblical truth through these two as they struggled with some of the same things I encountered.

During my teen years I found devotional books written for teenagers. In each season of my life, God directed me toward material that eventually helped me realize that the Bible was the greatest devotional ever written.

But don't lose heart if you didn't start a spiritual investment in your daughter when she was young. You can begin right now!

And now that your daughter has made a commitment to Christ, what's next? You'll want to help her grow in her faith! And you'll want to pray that God will give her a deep thirst for His Word. You'll also want to make Christ a regular part of your conversations.

If your daughter is a new Christian, it may take a while for the two of you to get comfortable with spiritual discussions. Even if the two of you have been Christians for some time now, maybe you still don't have many spiritual discussions. To help ground your daughter spiritually, it's important that faith become a consistent part of your everyday conversation.

THE BASICS

Praying together before meals is a great place to start spiritual discussions. If you're not in the habit of thanking God for your food, start doing so. Simply say something like, "Hey, before we dig in, let's just take a second to thank God for the fact that we have food to eat and a home to live in." And then offer a simple prayer. After you've done this consistently for a couple weeks—and your family has come to expect it—begin asking other family members if they'd like to offer thanks for the meal.

Then consider time alone with your daughter for prayer. Try

stepping into her bedroom at night before she turns out her light. Sit on the edge of her bed and ask her questions that require more than a yes or no answer. "Honey, if you could change anything about today, what would it be?" Or "What's the most frustrating thing going on in your life right now?" And then follow up with "Let's pray about that."

You, as her mom, will need to take the initiative to pray. Don't expect her to join you at first (unless she's a strong Christian and the two of you are used to doing this). Take the initiative and pray for her. Thank God for giving you this beautiful girl, and lift her needs and frustrations to Him.

After doing this for a couple of months, you'll begin to grow closer to your daughter. She may not tell you she looks forward to these times together, but you're actually giving her a lot of security by doing this.

How is this providing security? you may be thinking.

You're actually walking your daughter into the throne room of heaven every time you pray with her. That's security! It gives a teen confidence to hear her mom praying for her and with her at night and to know she's praying for her throughout her day as well.

After a few months of praying with her, ask her to begin praying as well. If she's uncomfortable with that, challenge her to simply pray a one-sentence prayer: "God, thanks for today."

And gradually encourage her to increase that to a three-sentence prayer. Give her specific things to pray about: your family, school, her future, health concerns, etc.

PRAY EVERYWHERE

Of course, by her bed at nighttime isn't the only place you can pray with your daughter. Teach her that you can pray anywhere and everywhere. Help her learn that there's absolutely nothing too big and nothing too small for her to pray about. If it concerns her, God cares about it!

I was fortunate to grow up in a family that had prayer time often. I can remember times my dad would get up, turn the TV off (because we didn't have remote controls when I was a kid), and say, "Let's kneel as a family and pray together."

My brother would kneel by the couch, I'd kneel by the piano bench, Dad by the recliner, and Mom by her chair. We'd go around the circle and pray about whatever was on our minds.

Did we do this every night? No. Mom and Dad wanted us to know that we needed our own individual prayer times as well, but the times that we knelt together as a family have been imprinted on my mind, and I'll never forget them! It taught me the importance of prayer. If Mom and Dad thought praying together was more important than the TV show we were watching, it must be pretty important!

ON PAPER

Another great way of helping your daughter grow spiritually is by developing a prayer journal together. Take the initiative to start a notebook and list some of your prayer requests on the first page. Pass it off to your daughter and ask her to list her concerns in the notebook as well. Pray together about these requests, and place a date by them when you've received an answer to your prayers.

One section might include a list of people you can begin praying for who aren't Christians. Another section may contain a creative ongoing list of things you're thankful for (chocolate is on my list!), and you might want to fill another section with favorite Scriptures. By passing it back and forth between you, you're keeping each other aware of the most important things in your lives—the things you're taking to God.

HER OWN BIBLE

Take your daughter Bible shopping. This should be a fun experience the two of you enjoy together. There are Bibles on the market for every season of our lives: Bibles for children, Bibles for teens, Bibles for couples, Bibles for families.

Look through several different versions and lots of different styles. I think student Bibles are great for teens! They're full of eye-catching graphics, a variety of Scripture helps to aid in understanding what you've read, and lots of extras. Make sure, however, that she gets a version that's easy to understand, not simply a Bible that looks cool. Spend some time reading favorite passages in several different ones, and ask her which one she thinks is easiest to understand. When she's found one she really loves, purchase it as a special gift for her. Write a note to her inside the front cover and include one of your favorite verses.

You may also want to purchase some Bible markers—pens or colored pencils specially designed to not bleed through thin paper—and tell her to mark up her Bible. Tell her to underline verses that stand out to her, and to place a question mark in the margin of something she reads but doesn't understand. That will remind her to ask someone about it later.

Also, encourage her to find a "life verse" for herself—a Scripture that has significant meaning and will carry her through the good times and the hard times. Give her a special pen to write that verse in the front of her Bible. Let her know there's no hurry to find this verse; it may take a while. That's okay. The issue isn't when she gets it; the issue is that she finds a verse that has special meaning from God directly to her heart. She'll know it when she finds it.

Make sure you have a life verse for yourself that you can share with your daughter as she seeks for her own.

READING THE BIBLE

Once she has her own Bible, encourage her to read it consistently. I always tell teens to read the Bible every single day—even if it's just *one minute* a day! Why is that important?

1. It helps us to develop discipline in turning to God's Word.
2. It teaches us that God's Word is of utmost importance in our lives.
3. It establishes a good habit. After that habit has been formed, our reading the Bible will become something automatic that we do regularly. Like breathing, reading the Bible will simply become an essential part of our lives.

After she has become accustomed to reading her Bible one minute a day, it will become something she looks forward to and grows dependent on, and her one minute will eventually turn into much more. But if you tell her to start with a large goal—say half an hour every day—she may begin with excitement, but she'll gradually lose heart when she misses the mark a few times. Rather than have her become discouraged and throw in the towel, motivate her with a goal she knows she can reach. Anyone can read the Bible for one minute a day!

If she doesn't know where to begin, suggest the gospel of John. After that, encourage her to read Proverbs. There are thirty-one chapters in Proverbs, so she can read one chapter every day for an entire month. After that, grab another gospel account: Matthew. Then dig into the Psalms. Then back to the New Testament.

There's really no right or wrong way to read the Bible. Any way we read it is correct, because the entire thing is God revealing himself to us. There are some one-year Bibles available that have a reading plan geared to move you through the entire Bible in a year. But if you don't want to invest in a one-year Bible, here's a little secret my dad shared with me when I was in the fourth grade.

He said, "Susie, if you read three chapters of the Bible every single day and read five chapters every Sunday, you'll have automatically read the entire Bible in one year." That's a good plan. And everyone ought to read through the Bible a few times in their lives.

My pastor encourages our congregation to read through the Bible each year, and at the end of the year he offers a free pizza party for everyone who accomplished their goal. I decided to toss some creativity into my Bible reading, so I read it on my knees one year. It took on a special meaning as I read my three chapters each day and five on Sunday while on my knees. It was a humbling experience and kept my focus on how small I am and how great He is. Being on our knees puts things in proper perspective very quickly.

Another year I decided to read the Bible through out loud. I also strive to read a different version than the one I read the year before. It's interesting to read the same passages that are stated a little differently in another version. Some Scriptures seem to stand out as never before simply because I'm reading them in a version I'm not so familiar with.

But again, it's not really important *how* we read the Bible; it's simply important that we read it!

SPIRITUAL HELPS

A couple of things that will help your daughter grow in her faith are good devotional books written specifically for teens and Bible studies geared to her age group. I've written several of both, and you can view them on my Web site, *www.CloserMomsandDaughters.com*.

While a devotional book won't take the place of the Bible, it can enhance her quiet time with the Lord. And an interactive Bible study will take her through a specific book of the Bible and help her understand what's being said and how it applies to her life right now.

I know several moms who lead a teen girl's Bible study in their home once a week for their daughter and her friends. What a great way to get to know who she's hanging out with and be a positive influence at the same time!

WHAT ABOUT CHURCH?

I believe church attendance and involvement are crucial to spiritual growth. I know many will disagree with that statement, thinking, *I can worship God anywhere! I don't have to be inside a building to feel close to Him.*

While that's certainly true, the benefits of plugging into a local body of believers are many compared with trying to create your own private church experience.

Here are some reasons plugging into a church is important:

It Gives You a Place to Serve

Once you've found a church you believe God has led you to, you'll have a variety of ways to minister and serve others. The apostle James tells us that faith without works is dead. Good works certainly don't save us—God's grace saves us. But once we've given our lives to Him and have established a relationship with Him, God will begin to talk with us about getting involved in good works. He wants us to give and serve and edify the church.

It Provides Accountability

When you're involved in church, people notice if you're not there. To know others are counting on you to be there helps provide motivation to attend consistently. And as you become more involved with the people within the church, you'll begin to share your needs and prayer requests with them. They can gently hold you accountable.

It Allows You to Be a Witness

Your very presence at church ministers to others. When I see some of the senior citizens hobble into my church with their walkers and there's snow on the ground, I'm inspired! Just the fact that they're there ministers to me!

It Gives You Perspective

Yes, you can grow spiritually on your own by reading the Bible and praying, but you need other people to challenge what you're thinking and absorbing. Plugging into church gives you the much-needed perspective from spiritual leaders to keep you on the right track spiritually. A pastoral staff and other believers will offer more than your own interpretation of what God is saying to you.

YOUR DAUGHTERS AND CHURCH

When should your daughters start going to church? I hope you'll actually bring them up in church. In other words, as soon as you're able to get up and get out after their births, I hope you'll be in church *with* your daughters.

But if this hasn't been your history, don't lose heart! You can start right now! Parents often ask, "What if my daughter doesn't want to go to church?"

I'll respond to this with three answers:

1. You're the parent! And the age-old statement still applies. As long as she's living under your roof, she abides by your rules. If you say we're going to church, we're going to church!

2. Show her how important church is to you by your own involvement, words, and actions. We naturally talk about the things we love. Fall in love with your church and the people in it,

and she'll see your excitement about how rewarding it is to be plugged into a body of believers.

3. Find out *why* she doesn't want to attend church. Perhaps the church you've selected doesn't have a youth group. Just as it's important for you to get involved and make Christian friends at church, it's even more important for your daughter. The needs of your children should take precedence over yours.

If the church you've selected doesn't have a good youth program and the church across town does (and you agree with their theology, etc.), then by all means join the church that can best meet the needs of your children. I've seen a lot of families lose their children to the world simply because they never had a place to plug in at church.

Make sure the church you're attending has a variety of ways to minister to your kids through discipleship, social activities, and areas of service.

CHURCH IS WHERE THE FAMILY IS

If you're looking for a new church, make it "family business." Involve everyone in your family with this important decision. Gather together for prayer and ask God to guide you. You'll want to visit several different churches—and it may take a while—before you finally settle on one specific one.

Perhaps you're wondering, *What if my husband and I love church A, but our daughter wants to go to church B?* Again, if you can agree with the theology of church B, and if your daughter is excited about ministry there, be willing to put your own desires aside and go where your daughter will be spiritually fed.

At some point, after your daughter has left home, she'll make her own decision about where to attend church—or whether she'll attend at all. But meanwhile, make church membership and involvement a priority for your family. It's crucial to your daughter's spiritual growth.

WHAT A PARENT CANNOT DO

I can share your life . . .
>   but I cannot live it for you.

I can teach you things . . .
>   but I cannot make you learn.

I can give you directions . . .
>   but I cannot always be there to lead you.

I can allow you freedom . . .
>   but I cannot account for it.

I can take you to church . . .
>   but I cannot make you believe.

I can teach you right from wrong . . .
>   but I cannot always decide for you.

I can make you beautiful clothes . . .
>   but I cannot make you lovely inside.

I can offer you advice . . .
>   but I cannot accept it for you.

I can give you love . . .
>   but I cannot force it upon you.

I can teach you to be a friend . . .
>   but I cannot make you one.

I can teach you to share . . .
>   but I cannot make you unselfish.

I can teach you respect . . .
>   but I cannot force you to show honor.

I can advise you about friends . . .
>   but I cannot choose them for you.

I can teach you about sexual purity . . .
>   but I cannot keep you pure.

I can tell you about drinking and drugs . . .
>   but I cannot say no for you.

I can let you work . . .
>   but I cannot make you responsible.

I can teach you to obey . . .
>   but I cannot answer for your actions.

I can teach you kindness . . .
    but I cannot force you to be gracious.
I can warn you about sin . . .
    but I cannot make you moral.
I can love you as a child . . .
    but I cannot place you in God's family.
I can pray for you . . .
    but I cannot make you walk with God.
I can teach you about Jesus . . .
    but I cannot make Him your Savior.
I can show you faith . . .
    but I cannot make you trust in Christ.
I can teach you about prayer . . .
    but I cannot make you pray.
I can tell you how to live . . .
    but I cannot give you eternal life.

—Author Unknown

Chapter 4

PROMOTING PURITY

Purity in your daughter's life actually begins with you. Does that put your stomach in knots? It shouldn't. Perhaps there are some things in your past that you're not proud of. Or maybe you became a Christian later in life and regret some mistakes you made years ago. Please remember that if you've sought forgiveness from God, He holds no record of your past! *You* are the best teacher for sexual purity your daughter can have. Let's take a peek at one mom and daughter's story.

DIANE AND KYM

Diane's teen daughter was seventeen, and like most girls her age, she was interested in dating. Diane and her husband agreed that Kym could date guys from their church and possibly other churches.

"Kym came home bubbling about a guy in her science class," Diane says. "He wanted to take her to a basketball game."

Diane encouraged her daughter to bring church into their conversation, and to find out more about him. "She said he didn't go to church, but he was a nice guy," Diane says. "I was afraid to let her go out with him."

Diane was fearful for a good reason.

Any guy who doesn't have a strong relationship with God should be off limits in a dating relationship with your daughter. Am I being strict? Yes. But stay with me. There's a reason.

Pornography has become a huge part of the lives of teens. Studies show that one in three guys are heavy porn users.[1]

In a survey of Internet users aged ten to seventeen, 42 percent said they had seen online pornography in a recent twelve-month span. In the same survey, more than one-third of sixteen- and seventeen-year-old boys said they had intentionally visited X-rated sites in the past year.[2]

Guys who don't have a relationship with Christ don't have a moral reason to reject pornography. Christian teen guys struggle with this issue as well, but most have a sense that what they're doing is wrong, and they are more likely to receive help due to their relationship with Christ.

Bottom line: Your daughter needs to be extremely selective when accepting a date (and this is something you'll want to teach her). Chances are high that a non-Christian is involved in unacceptable behavior—whether it's pornography or something else—and your daughter is making unwise choices if she begins to date him.

WHAT DIANE KNEW

Diane knew well the problems that arise from dating someone who isn't a believer. "When I was eighteen, I began dating a guy from school who wasn't a Christian. I came from a Christian family who was

---

[1] Thompson, Sonya. University of Alberta Study, 5 March 2007, *www.healthnews-stat .com/?id=450&keys=porn-rural-teens.*

[2] Wolak, Janis, et al. "Unwanted and Wanted Exposure to Online Pornography in a National Sample of Youth Internet Users." Pediatrics 119 (2007); 247–257.

very involved in church. I was active in our youth group, and I hadn't planned on dating someone who didn't share my faith.

"But Danny was a nice guy from school who paid attention to me and made me feel special. We became friends because we both played in the percussion section of our school band."

One day after practice, Danny asked Diane if she'd like to grab a pizza with him. "It seemed so innocent. Even though I had determined to date only Christians, no Christian guys had asked me out. Getting a pizza after band practice didn't even seem like a real date."

After pizza, they went their separate ways, and it really didn't seem like a big deal. Two weeks later, Danny asked her out for a movie and dinner on a Saturday night. Her parents weren't crazy about the idea because they didn't know Danny. Diane promised to bring him inside the house to meet her family, and they agreed to let her go.

"I was thinking maybe I could talk him into coming to church with me the next morning. We had a great time, but he said he wasn't interested in church. That's when I should have said I couldn't go out with him anymore."

But they enjoyed each other's company, and they continued to talk. On their third date, Diane took off her winter gloves and opened Danny's glove box to put them inside. "I couldn't believe it! He had a rolled up *Playboy* inside. I felt sick to my stomach.

"I asked him about it, and he just said all the guys read them. I knew my convictions about dating non-Christians were something I should stick to and that I had made a big mistake by going out with him. That night—even though it was only our third date—he kissed me good-night. And while he was doing that, he slipped his hands underneath my blouse and began feeling me.

"I bolted away from him and told him that I couldn't date him anymore. He called me a goody-goody. It hurt my feelings; this was my friend! This was the guy I'd laughed with all year in the drum line, the guy I'd been to tons of football and basketball games with because of the band. How could he treat me like this?"

Diane later learned from other girls that Danny went even farther physically with them than he had with her. According to rumor, he was sleeping with several girls and had even gotten one pregnant.

"As I looked back on it, I realized that what Danny was feeding his mind with didn't leave just because he was on a date with a Christian girl. He had filled his head with porn, and when we were together, he was viewing me as he had viewed the girls in the magazine."

YOUR DAUGHTER

When your daughter is on a date, you don't want the guy she's with to be inserting her face into the obscene images in his mind. You want the guy she's with to treat her like the princess she is. You want him to be a godly role model and to put his relationship with Christ before everything else.

And though this story was about a non-Christian guy, the fact is that Christian guys also struggle with porn (as do Christian girls!). So I'm not suggesting that by dating only Christian guys your daughter will escape the damage that pornography can bring into a relationship. You'll want to pray with her for God's discernment, wisdom, and guidance regarding every dating option she has! Your goal is for her to date a godly guy who hasn't allowed porn to influence how he treats the opposite sex.

Yes, I want that for her . . . but there aren't any guys who fit that description in our small town, you may be thinking.

Okay. But is that a reason to compromise?

No.

If there aren't any godly young men in your area who will treat your daughter as a princess of God's kingdom, then the alternative is for her to do things with large groups of friends (no one-on-one dates) and to simply wait until God does bring the right guy into her life.

That might not happen until she's in college, or until she has established a career, or until she's involved as a single woman in a church away from home. This is where you, as her mom, have to trust her to God's provision.

DIANE'S EXPERIENCE

Diane looks back on the few dates she had with Danny as a failure. "I definitely didn't use good judgment. Yes, I got out when I should have, but I shouldn't have even started the relationship. I regret that."

When her daughter, Kym, started to date—and was interested in a guy from school who didn't attend church—Diane imagined her story being relived through her daughter.

"I didn't want Kym dating a nonbeliever like I did. There were too many risks. I didn't want her to have any regrets, I wanted her to live a life of purity."

Diane and her husband decided to take their daughter out to dinner and present her with a purity ring.

It was a special night. Her dad gave her flowers, and they went to a fancy Italian restaurant. Walt handed Kym the gift-wrapped box and said, "Kym, now that you're old enough to start dating, we want you to understand the importance of sexual purity. And when we talk about sexual purity, we're not just talking about having sex," he explained. "Purity is a lifestyle."

"It's everything you do," Diane said. "It's affected by the movies you watch, the way you dress, flirtatious actions, the people you hang out with."

"And this ring symbolizes your commitment to sexual purity. We're so proud of the pledge you've made to God to keep yourself sexually pure until your wedding night," Walt said. "But until then, you're going to be bombarded with opportunities almost every single day to compromise your purity."

"Every day?" Kym asked. "What do you mean?"

"Let's say Maria suggests you see an R-rated movie," Diane said. "Your purity will be affected by what you see on the screen."

"Or when you're invited to a party where you know drinks will be served," Walt continued. "You may think there's no harm because you won't be drinking, but, honey, your purity will be affected because you've chosen to put yourself in an unholy environment and surround yourself with people who don't share your standards for purity."

Kym held the black velvet box in her hands and ran her fingers over the smooth lid.

"And when you're trying on clothes in the mall," Diane said, "you know what our standards are. You know what pleases the Lord and what pleases us. So to wear something too low, too tight, too short, or too revealing goes against a lifestyle of purity."

"Honey, I wish you could see yourself how we see you. To us, you're a gold mine. You're the world's greatest treasure! And that's exactly how God sees you too," Walt said. "So to let anyone mar or chip the treasure is putting a dent in your purity."

"I like it that you think I'm a treasure," Kym said.

"You *are*, Kym. We don't just *think* it; we *know* it. That's reality," Diane explained.

"So this means your expectations of who you date should be extremely high," Walt added. "Because you are a treasure, you should only go out with guys who know that too. Guys who will treat you as such."

"But what does that mean?" Kym pressed.

Walt didn't miss a beat. "A treasure, Kim, is something that's not to be pawed over. It's not something that's passed around and touched all the time. Think of it this way: You walk inside a museum and see a giant diamond inside a glass box with a lock on it. Maybe there's a special light situated to accent the color and shape. People walk by and admire it, but they're not allowed to pick it up and pass it down the line. No one's allowed to touch it. It's too special. It's carefully guarded. That's how you need to think of yourself. You're *that* special!"

"I never thought of myself that way," Kym admitted.

"Well, again, this is reality, and this is how you need to see yourself," Diane emphasized.

Kym slowly opened the velvet box, gasped with delight, and carefully removed the ring from the box.

Walt reached his hands toward his daughter. "May I?" Kym placed the ring in his hands, and he slipped the ring on her finger. "Kym," he said, "this is a reminder of your commitment to purity to God, to your parents, and to your future husband. Every time you feel this metal against your flesh, let it always remind you of the treasure you are and the high value placed on your purity."

As the three enjoyed dessert, they discussed dating, boundaries, and the kind of man they hoped Kym would marry someday.

"In the end, Kym didn't go out with the guy from science class. In fact, she never even asked to date during the rest of her high school experience. Things changed that night. She set her sights on dating a godly man who would treat her as the treasure she is.

After high school, she enrolled in a Christian college and started dating some Christian guys. By her senior year she had met the guy she knew she never wanted to live without. They were married a year after college graduation, and he has always treated her as the princess her parents knew she was.

On Kym's wedding night, she presented Max with the purity ring her parents had given her in high school. "This simple ring," she said, "has been the symbol of me saving myself wholly . . . completely . . . just for you. It's yours now, and I'm so happy to be able to give it to you and you alone."

BOTTOM LINE

It all boils down to the fact that your greatest desire is for your daughter to become all God dreams for her. A big part of His dream is that she live a sexually pure lifestyle. After your daughter has made a commitment to remain sexually pure until marriage, how can you help her maintain that commitment? In other words, how can you encourage purity success? Let's use the word SUCCESS and spell out a strategy.

S: Start now. Now matter how young or old your daughter is, purity can begin right now! Remember, sexual purity isn't simply saying no to intercourse; it involves every area of our lives. So help her make wise media choices. Guide her in selecting modest yet fashionable clothing. Be her mentor.

U: Understand there's a high calling on your life. Help your daughter know that God dreams big dreams for her (Jeremiah 29:11; Ephesians 3:20), and He calls her to holiness (1 Peter 1:15–16). That means—with the help of the Holy Spirit inside her—she can soar above the crowd.

C: Clarify your boundaries. Help your daughter know her boundaries before she ever goes on her first date. Trying to figure out what her limits are while she's in the backseat of a car isn't good timing. Discuss boundaries together. What's the line? Holding hands? A kiss on the cheek?

C: Create your own success story. Help your daughter realize that she's in control of her sexual purity success. She can write her own story. God will empower her to keep the commitment she's made, and she can be successful with it.

E: Expect flak. Remind her that her non-Christian friends won't understand why she has such high standards. That's okay. We don't expect the world to understand. Again, she has a high calling on her life. She may get made fun of. Prepare her for this. Christ said the world would hate us, but He also reminded us that it hated Him as well.

S: State your convictions. When she's dating, it's important that she's able to articulate her values and standards. She should be able to share *what* she believes about purity and *why* she has adopted this as a lifestyle.

S: Seek like-minded friends. It's easier to maintain convictions when surrounded by others who share the same values. Encourage your daughter to be selective when dating and even when choosing close friends.

Chapter 5

WHAT ABOUT FAILURES?

Perhaps like Diane in chapter 4, you have some past memories you're not fond of. Are you wondering if you should share your past with your daughter? And how much should you share? Are there things you definitely shouldn't share?

Use these suggestions as guidance when trying to make those decisions:

Is It Necessary to Teach a Lesson?

Could Diane help her daughter know the importance of dating only Christians without telling her daughter about the past? Maybe. Perhaps all Kym needed to hear were current statistics on porn, drugs, drinking, and other activities that many teens are involved in. Maybe all she needed was a good discussion with Mom reminding her that even though she was friends with this guy, she didn't really know what he did outside of school (alcohol, gambling, porn).

Diane tried discussing the issues with her daughter, but Kym wasn't convinced. "He's not like that. I just know it," she said. So Diane decided to share her own experience with Kym.

Will It Make Someone Else in Your Family Look Bad?

If what you have to share will demean your husband or another family member to your daughter, it's unlikely you need to share this portion of your past in such detail. Even if you're able to share it without mentioning the other family member, think twice.

Doris and Cliff married right after college graduation. She didn't know that he'd been exposed to pornography as a child, but after they'd been married a few years, he shared his struggle with her. Doris and Cliff sought counseling, and though it took several years, Cliff finally discovered victory in this area of his life.

When their daughter, Jill, began to get serious about the Christian guy she was dating in college, her parents both stressed to her that it was important Jill and Cody be open with each other about their pasts.

"Why?" Jill said. "Cody's a Christian. He's totally in love with God. I don't care about what happened before he met Christ."

The next day, as Jill and Doris were shopping, Doris began to share about Cliff's introduction to pornography when he was a child. "Your dad didn't actively seek it, honey," she explained, "but other boys got him involved. I didn't know this before we were married. I wish I had known, because we could have dealt with it before we were married. He's free now, but we really struggled through some tough years because of this. So please ask Cody to be very open with you about his past and anything that could be a struggle should the two of you get married."

Though Doris meant well, Jill's view of her dad was never the same. She felt funny whenever he wanted to hug her. She hated herself for feeling this way, but she couldn't get past the fact that he'd once struggled with pornography.

Should Doris have shared this with her daughter? No. It made her husband look bad. Even though he now has victory, Doris planted seeds of doubt regarding Cliff in Jill's mind.

If sharing past failures with your daughter will make another family member look bad, resist the urge to share.

Will What You Share Cause Your Daughter to Lose Respect for You?

No matter how sordid your past may be, if your daughter can see that your life now is holy, she'll probably marvel at all God has done in your life. If, however, she's not able to see a huge change from your past to your present, think twice about sharing. Chances are high that she won't respect you for it.

When Fran was in middle school, she was introduced to alcohol at a party she attended one Friday night after a football game. From that point on, it almost seemed as though Fran was "genetically wired" to become an alcoholic. She had several drinks that first night, and the next day she found some older friends who were drinking and were willing to share. Fran quickly became dependent on alcohol, and by the time she was fifteen, she was a full-blown alcoholic.

She continued to party, and she soon added marijuana and pills to her drinking. She dropped out of school at sixteen and continued a downward spiral. A friend she worked with encouraged Fran to attend Alcoholics Anonymous and even volunteered to go with her.

Fran finally went—just to get her co-worker off her back. But once she heard the success stories of others like herself, she decided she wanted her life back. Of course, it wasn't easy, but Fran was finally able to give up drinking and drugs.

Well . . . almost. Let's fast-forward seventeen years. Fran is now married with a teen daughter of her own. Though Fran doesn't drink often, she still has a glass of wine now and then. When she found out her daughter, Rebekah, wanted to attend a questionable party, Fran was immediately reminded of her past. To make a strong case for why Rebekah shouldn't go, Fran decided to share her past.

Rebekah was blown away. She'd never known her mom didn't have a high school diploma, was a former alcoholic, or had messed around with drugs.

When Fran finished sharing her personal story, she expected Rebekah to understand why attending the party wasn't a wise choice. Instead, Rebekah surprised her with a different response.

"You're still struggling, aren't you, Mom? I mean, if you'd really kicked alcohol, you wouldn't go near a drink now. But you drink on every holiday and sometimes after work just to calm your nerves. You may not be an alcoholic anymore, but you're still drinking. If you can do it and get by, so can I."

Fran's plan totally backfired. Because she hadn't experienced complete victory in this area of her life, her daughter lost respect for her.

Again, before you share your past with your daughter, make sure you're living right. If she sees a change in your present from the past you're sharing, she'll listen. If not, you risk the possibility of losing her respect.

Is There a Definite Reason to Share?

Some people simply talk too much. Don't share your past just to be talking. Determine first if there's a need that can be met between you and your daughter by sharing your past. If not, don't share it.

Felicia falls into this category. She's uncomfortable with silence, so she constantly fills it with her own voice. I can't be around her more than two minutes before I'm looking for an escape route. I don't know if her daughter feels the same way; maybe Cheyenne is just used to it.

But two years ago in December, when the two of them were shopping for Christmas gifts, the conversation turned to marriage. "How did you know that Dad was the one for you?" Cheyenne asked in the crowded mall.

"I just knew. And of course, I'd prayed about it. But my heart just told me he was the one." At that point, Felicia would have done well to stop and allow her daughter to ask another question. Perhaps Cheyenne was thinking about her own future and wondering about the man she'd marry someday.

But because Felicia's a talker and is insecure with silence, she continued when she shouldn't have.

"Of course, even though you know someone's right for you, that doesn't mean marriage will be easy. Your dad and I have sure had some rough spots. Six years into our marriage, I walked out on him. I just wasn't sure I wanted to be married anymore."

What?! Cheyenne was thinking. *My mom left my dad?*

Though there was no reason to share that information with her daughter, and though it served no benefit at all, Felicia just kept talking.

Though Cheyenne and her mom have a good relationship, Cheyenne has confided in me that she struggles with a gnawing doubt in her soul . . . always wondering if her mom will simply get tired of her life and walk out on the family. She doesn't fully trust her mom as she once did.

Should Felicia have shared this with her daughter? No. It didn't do any good, and it planted doubt and mistrust in Cheyenne's mind. Don't talk simply to talk. Learn to be comfortable with silence. And when your daughter is asking the questions, answer and then let her process that information in the silence between the two of you and see if she wants to continue asking questions. A wise mom knows how to listen and read between the lines instead of simply filling silence with words.

Can God Be Glorified?

As in everything you do, you want your heavenly Father to be lifted up. Will He receive glory by what you have to share with your daughter?

My friend Gary is an evangelist. He travels around the nation several times a year, sharing how God delivered him from a life of drugs in his younger years. Gary was a popular nightclub singer, and partly because of his grandmother's refusal to stop praying for him, he finally surrendered his life to Christ.

His children know about his past and can see how God so wonderfully uses it to bring glory to His kingdom. As Gary preaches and sings and brags on God, people are won to the Lord. God is definitely being glorified in spite of his past.

In this situation, it was wise to let his family know of his past, and it was essential to let them know so he could involve himself in public ministry. But the bottom line is this: God is glorified through his sharing.

Hopefully that's your goal as well: to bring glory to Christ in everything you do. If sharing your past with your children won't glorify the Lord, don't share it.

In every situation, pray about your past. Ask God for His wisdom and discernment. Tell Him you only want to share if it's His will. Then trust Him to let you know what to do. He's faithful! He'll not only let you know *if* you should share your past, but He'll also let you know *when* to share it.

Chapter 6

WHEN SHE'S THIRTY

In chapter 1, we discussed the fact that your daughter is closely watching your life. She *will* copy pieces of your lifestyle. Which pieces of your lifestyle do you want your daughter to imitate?

In thinking about this, it's obvious you have to think about right now. But I also challenge you to think about the future. And guess what—it starts now!

Decide which areas of your life you want your daughter to imitate, and begin living out those areas loudly right now. For example, if you want her to imitate your savvy budgeting skills when she's thirty and has her own family, she needs to see you demonstrating those skills today.

What kind of woman do you want your daughter to be when she's eighteen? When she's twenty-five? When she's thirty?

Think about it.

In fact, grab a pen and get serious. (I totally believe in marking up books. You should see my Bible!)

Take a moment to think ahead and jot some things down. Let's start with high school graduation, or when your daughter turns eighteen.

GRADUATION

At eighteen years of age, how do you want your daughter to view herself?

As she enters college (probably at eighteen), or as she enters the work force, what goals do you want her to have?

How do you want her to feel about money (tithing, budgeting, saving, spending)?

What criteria do you hope she uses when choosing a roommate?

What criteria do you want her to use when she selects a church?

Where do you want her to be spiritually at this point?

What are some of her natural talents that will have surfaced by age eighteen?

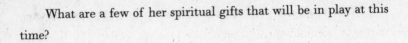

What are a few of her spiritual gifts that will be in play at this time?

What qualities do you want her to seek in a dating relationship?

What's the most difficult thing in her life *right now* that you sincerely hope she overcomes by age eighteen?

REAL LIFE

Twelve-year-old Kendall Waddey had no idea that a trip with her mom to Nashville would change her life. With stops and layovers along the way, Kendall couldn't help but notice that most people's suitcases were black and gray, and basically pretty dull.

"When I grow up," she told her mom, "I want to design luggage that's fun, something really cool!"

Because her mom knew her daughter's strengths and gifts, she encouraged her not to wait until she was grown. Her mom shared Kendall's dream with her husband, and Kendall's parents both encouraged her to get busy.

In essence, they were planning when Kendall was age twelve for what she could be doing when she was thirty. I met Kendall when she was fourteen. At the time of this book's release, she's sixteen, and she has an entire line of luggage called Like Luggage (*www .likeluggage.com*).

Her Web site boasts: "Like is not just luggage, it's an attitude." Kendall has mixed greens on pinks, yellows on pinks, black and pink, orange and yellows, blues and pinks . . . She's developed exactly what she dreamed of: an amazingly cool line of luggage that looks and screams excitement.

That's what this question-and-answer exercise is all about. It's to encourage you to think *now* about what kinds of things you hope your daughter will be doing in the future. Let's keep moving!

MID-TWENTIES AND WORKING

Let's fast-forward to when your daughter is twenty-five. She's probably in her first full-time job. Still have your pen? Keep writing!

What kind of work ethic do you want to observe in her life at age twenty-five?

How do you hope she responds to a difficult boss?

How would you like to see her deal with a job she doesn't like?

What kind of lifestyle do you desire for her to live in front of her co-workers?

What are some ways that you can foresee her being "Jesus with skin on" to those around her in the work force?

Your daughter may be married at this point, but let's pretend she's not. Let's just assume she's in a serious relationship. In what ways can you expect to see morality and holy standards echoed in her lifestyle with the man she's dating?

What kind of man do you hope she marries?

Is it enough that her serious boyfriend (or potential husband) is a Christian? Or do you want to be more specific?

How do you hope to see her handle conflict between the two of them?

REAL LIFE

Gloria and her daughter, Caitlyn, hit some rough spots during Caitlyn's teen years, but as she prepared for college and started to mature, the two began to develop a close relationship with each other. Because Caitlyn was moving several hundred miles away from home for college, Gloria wanted to maintain the closeness that had recently emerged between them and deepen it even more.

So she determined to do everything she could to let her daughter know she loved her and believed in her. At least once a month she sent her a care package filled with practical essentials: laundry detergent, shampoo, quarters for the washer and dryer. And a few times during the semester, she sent her a Wal-Mart gift card.

Gloria called often just to touch base and ask about classes, new friends, and how her part-time job at the campus library was going.

Caitlyn shared the difficulty of working for a much older boss who had run the library for years and was unwilling to implement new ideas. Gloria listened carefully and shared tips for getting along with someone who wasn't easy to work with. She thought of her own experience in her first job as a sales clerk in a large department store and shared with her daughter how she made her position bearable even though her boss was always cranky and often unfair.

Gloria made special cards for Caitlyn, listing several qualities she noticed in her daughter's life that would someday make her a great wife. Though she didn't date much during college, they discussed what qualities Caitlyn considered nonnegotiable with the man she would marry. Gloria and her daughter talked often about what would make a godly marriage strong and what could be stumbling blocks.

Gloria also sent Caitlyn special Scriptures to help her through the tough times she encountered in classes where professors weren't receptive to her faith.

Mom and daughter continued to deepen their relationship during

Caitlyn's college years. Gloria was excited to see her daughter accept a position with a ministry for teen girls following graduation.

Caitlyn met a young man on staff in the same ministry. He shared her passion for helping teens, and the two began a dating relationship. Because Gloria and her daughter had prepared in advance regarding non-negotiable qualities in a husband, what would make a strong marriage, etc., Caitlyn didn't struggle with many of the same doubts and questions her peers did when they were involved in serious relationships.

Gloria had already mentored her daughter—though much of it long distance—about how to be a great wife. She instilled within Caitlyn the importance of being her husband's greatest cheerleader. So although Caitlyn and Brad had disagreements during their dating relationship, they were soon solved because of the investment Gloria had made *ahead of time* in her daughter's life.

Brad and Caitlyn are now engaged and are excited about the future God has for both of them.

Again, moms, this is the benefit of answering these questions now. By doing so, it's forcing you to project you *and* your daughter into the future. Why is that important? It enables you to zero in on how you can prepare her *now* for the variety of stages in her life.

AND AT THIRTY . . .

Let's say your daughter is married and has a child. What qualities as a mother do you want to see reflected in her?

What importance to prayer and Bible-reading do you want to see between her, her husband, and her child?

What kind of church involvement do you hope to see in your daughter?

Do you want to see your daughter involved in ministry outside the home? (Besides her family, which is her greatest ministry.) If so, what kind of ministry would you like it to be, and what degree of involvement do you see for her?

How do you hope your daughter and her husband will handle their money? How important should the following be to her?

- Tithing
- Saving

- Paying bills on time
- Spending
- Family vacations
- Home furnishings
- Automobiles
- Adult sports (boat, motorcycle, learning to fly, skiing, fitness club, etc.)

What values do you want to see in your daughter's child?

REAL LIFE

Though Lucy and her husband provided a Christian home for their daughter Macie, neither ever thought about projecting themselves and their daughter into the future to discuss the kinds of things we're dealing with in this chapter.

Lucy is the life of every party—a really fun and creative mom. All four of her children were involved in church—as were she and her husband. Although all four of her children made a profession of faith during their childhood years, Lucy became concerned about Macie when she entered college.

Three of Lucy's children attended a Christian university, but Macie yearned for sorority life on the secular campus many of her friends planned to attend. Lucy and her husband consented to allow Macie to attend the university of her choice, but they never thought of discussing with her ahead of time the differences between a secular campus and a Christian one.

Long story short, Macie joined one of the most popular sororities on campus and began drinking and partying, but she maintained a high grade-point average and aced her classes. She was a popular girl on campus and dated several young men.

During her senior year, Macie fell in love with the man she knew she'd spend the rest of her life with. Much to Lucy's disappointment, the two began living together while saving up money for medical school. Though Lucy and her husband shared their concerns with their daughter, Macie argued that her life was going great and she was making smart decisions.

"My mind began playing tricks on me," Lucy says. "I should have done this, I should have done that. My thoughts were relentless. Should I have forced her to attend a Christian university—even though that wouldn't have guaranteed she would have maintained her faith? Should I not have allowed her to join a sorority?"

Let's fast-forward. Macie married the guy she was living with, both graduated from medical school, and they now have a thriving practice and three beautiful children.

I spent the weekend with Lucy not long ago, and she expressed concerns for her grandchildren. "Macie and Alan are great people," she said. "She's still the kindhearted, fun, creative, energetic person you knew as a little girl, Susie."

I took a moment to affirm Lucy and simply listened as she continued. "But they don't attend church anywhere. And their children are so materialistic. They have everything they want, and they have the very best of everything. Macie and Alan make lots of money, and they consider themselves Christians, but I'm worried. If they never attend church or associate with other Christians, and if they don't plug their children into church, I'm concerned about where they'll spend eternity."

Lucy and her husband maintain a close relationship with Macie and Alan. They baby-sit the children often and attempt to be the hands of Christ to them by serving and giving whenever the opportunity arises. But as I left her house, I'll never forget what she said: "Susie, their children attend a Christian school, and they've begged Macie and Alan to take them to church, but they say they just don't have the time."

Wow. That breaks my heart—especially because I've known Macie since she was eight months old. I'm proud of all she's accomplished in life, but I'm saddened she's not cultivating a personal spiritual life for her children.

Moms, there's no guarantee that by answering these questions and purposefully thinking ahead and determining to help guide your daughter's life that she'll respond in a spiritually positive way. But it does increase your chances.

Lucy and her husband were extremely involved in church *with* their children, yet Macie still chose to make choices opposite of the way she was brought up.

BACK TO NOW

Time to jump back into the present. How did it feel to view your daughter in the future? Did it frighten you? Excite you? Stress you? Confuse you?

Earlier we talked about setting yourself up to be the influencer in your daughter's life that she can imitate. You don't have to tell your daughter to watch you; she already is. And good or bad, she'll pick up some of you—your characteristics, a bit of your personality.

Just when you thought you were finished with that pen, I'm going to ask you to grab it again. Take this quick quiz to help determine the areas where you want your daughter to imitate you. Circle Yes if it's an area you'd like your daughter to duplicate; circle No if it's not.

Yes	No	How I handle the family budget
Yes	No	My emotional stability
Yes	No	My church involvement
Yes	No	How I treat my husband
Yes	No	How I treat my other family members
Yes	No	The relationship I have with my own mother
Yes	No	How I view men in general
Yes	No	My work ethic
Yes	No	My approach to ministry
Yes	No	How I view (or am involved in) missions
Yes	No	How I deal with correspondence (writing personal thank-you notes, returning phone calls, taking messages for other family members, etc.)
Yes	No	How I keep and maintain the home (including planning as well as cleaning)
Yes	No	My devotional life
Yes	No	How I handle conflict
Yes	No	How I express anger
Yes	No	How I take care of myself physically (including grooming as well as exercise and fitness)
Yes	No	My health
Yes	No	How I relate to those in authority
Yes	No	How I communicate with others
Yes	No	My spiritual life

AN HONEST LOOK

How'd you do? Are you surprised at the number of things in your life you do or don't want your daughter to replicate?

I hope you answered the questions honestly, because if you can objectively look at yourself and be gut-level honest about what you want to pass on to your daughter and what you need to improve, then you'll win your daughter, and you'll win the right to be heard.

What your daughter seeks from you most is honesty. Don't feel bad about having some areas in your life that you don't want your daughter to imitate. Again, being honest is the key. More than wanting you to be perfect in all areas of your life, your daughter wants your honesty.

It's okay to say, "Honey, I'm not great with numbers, so I'm hoping you'll rise above my ability to manage our household budget. I sometimes overspend in one area and have to borrow from another category to make up the difference. But it's something I'm working on."

That will shout volumes to your daughter, and it will also boost her own confidence if she *can* conquer math and become better at something than you are. (And who knows? You may need her to do your taxes someday!)

THE RIGHT TO BE HEARD

It seems that simply because you're the parent, you have the right to be heard. Unfortunately, it's not always that easy. Oftentimes you have to win the right to be heard. Yes, you're the parent, and you'll always be in charge (until she has left your home and is on her own), but you probably already know that responding to something with "Because I said so" just doesn't cut it.

How does one win the right to be heard? Let's start with what doesn't work:

Emphasizing Behavior Over Relationship

The most important ingredient in your relationship with your daughter is simply that: your relationship with your daughter! She needs to know beyond all doubt that you have placed the highest priority possible on your relationship with her.

When she fails the test, doesn't make the cheerleading squad, is kicked out of school, sneaks out and drinks, shoplifts, etc., she needs to know that while her behavior is unacceptable, it won't affect the relationship she has with you.

Ashley never dated in high school. When she began dating a great Christian guy during her junior year of college, her parents were thrilled. He was sharp and fun, and he treated Ashley like a princess.

When Ashley broke up with him, her parents were devastated—especially her mom. "What happened?" her mom asked. "Did you do something to make him mad?"

"No, Mom. *I* called it off."

"Why? Dustin's a great guy."

"It just wasn't right," she tried to explain.

"Ashley! What are you thinking? Dustin's a strong Christian, he treats you great, and he's majoring in accounting. He's perfect!"

"Mom, it just wasn't right."

"You've made a big mistake, Ashley. You'll never find another guy like Dustin."

Ashley was already hurting over the breakup with Dustin, but not having her mom's support hurt her even more. She never did share specific reasons with her mom for the breakup. And all she told her friends was, "I prayed about it, and I just knew he wasn't the guy God wanted me to spend the rest of my life with. He's wonderful; he really is. But I just don't see us together for a lifetime."

Her friends supported her, but her mom actually refused to speak with her for two weeks. Can you guess how open Ashley will be with her parents when she gets into another relationship?

Ashley needed something essential from her mom. She desperately needed to know that their relationship wouldn't change in spite of her actions. Ashley's mom finally came around, but Ashley is still guarded with her when discussing any type of relationship.

Putting More Stock in Outward Appearance Over Inward Progress

It's much easier to judge progress by what we see on the outside rather than how we're growing and developing on the inside, isn't it?

Fifteen-year-old Sydney had been chubby all her life. Now that she was in high school, her mom desperately wanted to help her drop a few pounds. She knew her daughter would probably want to get involved in athletics and would eventually start dating, so she suggested they try an exercise routine together.

Sydney began with enthusiasm. They started small by just walking around the block together a few times each evening. Then Sydney's mom increased their routine by adding some cardio exercises in their basement.

They both dropped a few pounds and were enthusiastic about the results. Sydney's mom took a close look at what she was feeding her family and decided she could make some healthy changes in their diet as well. Sydney did great at home, but when she was at school, her food choices weren't as healthy.

Mom continued to drop weight, but Sydney hit a plateau after losing ten pounds. Her mom couldn't understand it, so she began quizzing her daughter. "You've been faithful to maintain your exercise program at home. What's going on at school?"

Sydney explained that she had been assigned a late lunch period, and by the time she got to the cafeteria at one o'clock, she was starving. She admitted to grabbing a burger and fries and other food choices that weren't on her mom's approved list.

Her mom came unglued. "You have to be more careful, Sydney!"

she said. "You won't make the cheerleading squad at your current weight. And everyone knows that guys are attracted to smaller girls!"

Sydney was devastated and began to eat even more. Though she wasn't making the outward progress her mom wanted to see, Sydney actually had moved toward a healthier lifestyle by disciplining herself to exercise regularly and eat healthy at home.

If Mom had looked on the inside rather than the outside, she could have helped motivate her daughter to think healthy. She could have said, "Wow! That *is* a late lunch! Okay, let's beef up your breakfast, and let's pack a healthy snack for you to munch on between classes. When you get to the cafeteria it's okay to grab a burger and fries once in a while, but just try not to eat that way every day. Would it help if we packed your lunch?"

When Sydney's feeling down on herself because of her outer appearance, do you think she's going to open up with her mom when asked, "What's wrong, honey?"

PRACTICE MAKES PERFECT

We're all human, and it's understandable that you'll say things to your daughter that you wish you hadn't. When that happens, first go to God. He understands your humanity because He created you. Seek His forgiveness for saying things that hurt, and ask Him for wisdom and guidance.

Then approach your daughter and seek her forgiveness. I'm not talking about simply saying, "I'm sorry." I'm talking about going a step further and actually asking her to forgive you.

I wish Sydney's mom could have said something like, "Honey, I'm sorry. I should have thought before speaking. I sometimes get so focused on a specific goal that I get carried away. You really *have* made great progress! You've dropped an entire size. I'm proud of you. Will you forgive me for saying things that hurt your feelings? I sure love you, Sydney! And I want to remind you that you are a princess of the King of Kings! No matter what your weight is, God and I both will always be crazy in love with you."

THE WRONG WAY

We've chatted a bit about some incorrect ways to communicate, but let's quickly hit a few more common areas in which well-meaning moms can miss the mark by what they say.

- "Are you sure you want seconds?"
- "I'd hate for anyone we know to see you dressed like that."
- "I thought you were smarter than that!"
- "You don't need dessert."
- "Why don't you have a date for homecoming?"
- "I think your hair would look better if . . ."
- "I hate it when you wear that baseball cap."
- "What you're wearing doesn't make you look feminine."
- "You're wearing way too much makeup. Learn to do it right, or don't wear any at all."

WHAT TO SAY

Just as we quickly hit a few statements where well-meaning moms often miss the mark, let's cover a few examples of statements that can leave a positive impression on your daughters:

- "A few years from now, no one's going to remember who went to homecoming with whom. I believe the reason you haven't been asked is because guys know you have high standards and none of them measure up. So let's plan something really fun that night, okay? We'll do something that you'll remember forever."

- "I want to treat you to something extra special. I'm scheduling an appointment for us at the Clinique counter at the mall this Saturday morning. Their specialists will show us what looks best on our skin type and even how to apply it."
- "Want to go to (name of store) with me? I thought it would be fun to talk with the lady there who does body and color analysis. She can show us what styles will look best on our figures and which colors bring out our natural beauty."
- "Math was always hard for me too. I think with a little extra help from a tutor, you'll be fine."
- "The only way I can understand how you feel is if you tell me. I really do care about you. When you're ready to talk, I'm here."

MORE RIGHT STUFF

Now that we've talked about how *not* to win the right to be heard, let's chat about how you *can* earn that right. We've already touched on this some, but again, honesty will make you seem ten feet tall in your daughter's eyes.

Connie's daughter, Bryn, had always enjoyed going to church. But when Bryn turned fifteen, Connie began noticing some changes in her daughter's life. Bryn became more distant—shutting herself in her room more often. She wasn't as open at family dinner times, and she didn't have the same excitement about going to church.

When Connie asked her daughter what was going on, Bryn wouldn't open up. Connie didn't want to nag, but she was determined to find out what was happening with her daughter. So she tried a variety of things. She suggested they go shopping on Saturday, and Bryn only reluctantly agreed. Connie fixed Bryn's favorite meal, only to be met with, "I'm not very hungry."

Finally she suggested that her daughter invite some friends over on Friday evening. Bryn sarcastically remarked, "That'll take . . . like, two seconds."

Connie knew it was time to push, but to push gently. "What do you mean? You have all kinds of friends."

"That was middle school, Mom. High school's different."

Connie began naming a variety of girls that her daughter had hung out with the past year. One by one, Bryn explained what had happened.

"Aleisha's folks split, and she had to change schools. Kristy's got a boyfriend and spends all her time with him. Kathryn's drinking, and I don't wanna be with her. Abbie's a cheerleader now and has a whole group of new friends. Sam is in the gifted program and isn't on my track any longer. Brianna's still my friend, but she has mono and hasn't been to school for two weeks."

Connie's heart broke for her daughter. She wrapped her arms around Bryn as she tried to decide what to say. Her own teen years flashed in front of her face, and they weren't pleasant. *I don't want my daughter to know that I was never cool*, she thought. *But I also want her to know I can identify with not having friends.* Connie decided to go for it.

"Bryn, I was pretty much a geek when I was a teen."

Her daughter smiled slightly, and Connie admitted it felt good to see Bryn's face light up if only a little. "Seriously, I had one, maybe two really good friends throughout my entire high school experience."

"Why?"

"Well, I loved chemistry. I spent a lot of time after school in the lab, and there just weren't many girls who understood my interests. They were all busy chasing the cutest guy or reapplying their makeup in the bathroom while I was excited about doing extra-credit stuff."

Bryn actually laughed. Connie gave her daughter a squeeze. "So

I can understand what it's like to walk the halls alone. It doesn't feel good, does it?"

Bryn's eyes began to tear up, and Connie knew her vulnerability was paying off. "But, Bryn, there's Someone besides me who knows exactly how you feel, and that's Jesus. Think how alone He felt hanging on the cross. He was even temporarily separated from His own Father for our sins. Totally alone."

"Yeah, but that's Jesus. I'm not talking about dying for anyone. I'd just like to have someone to sit with during lunch."

"I know. Let's start praying together every single night that God will send you a special friend."

"You think it might happen in a week?" Bryn asked.

"Maybe. Maybe not. It might take longer than you want. But school just started three weeks ago. Don't you have that pole thing coming up pretty soon?"

"Mom!" Bryn smiled again. "It's not a pole thing. It's See You at the Pole. And yeah, it's always the fourth Wednesday in September. But what does that have to do with anything?"

"Isn't that where all the Christians get together and stand by your school's flagpole to pray for the school year?"

"Yeah. So?"

"So that's a great opportunity for you to find out who the other Christians are! Try to get the scoop on who's in charge, and make sure you're there. This is your chance to reach out to some other Christians who can become your friends."

Connie saw hope in her daughter's eyes that she hadn't seen in a while. "And in the meantime," she said, "we'll be praying specifically for some good Christian friends, okay?"

"Okay."

The two just sat together for a few minutes, and Connie thanked the Lord silently for helping her get through to her daughter.

Bryn finally spoke. "Mom?"

"Yeah, honey?"

"I'm glad you were a geek in high school."

"What?!"

"Well, think about it. If you weren't so smart, and if you hadn't taken your studies so seriously, we probably wouldn't have this great house and you wouldn't have the awesome job that you love."

Connie smiled and hugged her daughter. Being vulnerable had certainly paid off.

YOUR VULNERABILITY

Can you strive to become more vulnerable, more open, more honest with your daughter? If you can, you'll be earning the right to be heard. Again, your daughter doesn't care as much about you having everything all worked out in your life as she does about your genuineness and your honesty.

Time to grab that pen again! What are some areas in which you can be more vulnerable concerning your daughter? Go ahead—jot them down. When we make the effort to actually put something on paper, we get more serious about it!

HAND IN HAND

Honesty and vulnerability really go hand in hand. You can't be honest without being vulnerable. And you can't be vulnerable without being honest. As a mom, wouldn't you rather your daughter be honest with you instead of distancing herself and shutting down? And wouldn't you rather she share her vulnerability with you instead of putting on a good front? I'm assuming your answer is yes! And knowing that, you can imagine how much more she desires honesty and vulnerability from you! -

NEW ADDITION TO THE PERIODIC TABLE OF ELEMENTS

Element Name: WOMANIUM

Symbol: WO

Atomic Weight: (don't even go there)

Physical Properties: Generally soft and round in form. Boils at nothing and may freeze at any time. Melts when treated properly. Very bitter if not used well.

Chemical Properties: Very active. Highly unstable. Possesses strong affinity with gold, silver, platinum, and precious stones. Violent when left alone. Able to absorb great amounts of exotic food. Turns slightly green when placed next to a better specimen.

Usage: Highly ornamental. An extremely good catalyst for dispersion of wealth. Probably the most powerful income-reducing agent known.

Caution: Highly explosive in inexperienced hands.

—Colleen Narberth (used with permission)

Chapter 7

FILLING HER HEART

Success with boys starts in the heart. If your daughter's heart is full, she won't need a boy to fill it. And, as you know, teen girls fill their hearts with more than boys. The world is advertising all kinds of enticements to fill her heart: codependency, drugs, cutting, eating disorders, unhealthy friendships, inappropriate Internet use, alcohol, etc. But often during the teen years, her focus will be on boys. How can you fill your daughter's heart so that boys or other things from the world aren't the priority?

THE FATHER IN HER LIFE

Encourage your husband and daughter to begin having father-daughter dates. My friends Bill and Janice decided that before their daughter, Marie, began dating, her dad should be the one to set the standards for the type of guy she would date and how she should expect to be treated on a date.

So Janice helped Marie pick out a new dress for the occasion, and

Bill put on a suit and left the house while Marie got ready. He came back about an hour later and rang the doorbell for Marie. When she answered, he came inside the house, presented her with flowers, and sat down and chatted with Janice.

Bill wanted to show Marie that a guy worth dating won't honk the horn and expect her to walk out to his car. He'll come to the door, and he'll make time to come inside, sit down, and have an actual conversation with her parents.

Bill then told Marie's mom where they were going and when they'd be home. He opened all the doors for Marie, pulled out her chair once they were in the restaurant, and carried his part of the conversation. He asked her questions about herself. As he did, he explained that a guy worth dating won't simply talk about himself but will make an effort to get to know *her* by taking an active role in the conversation.

Throughout the evening, Bill explained to Marie that most guys her age wouldn't have the experience or life skills to do all that he was doing (maybe they wouldn't have the money to purchase flowers or to treat her to a nice restaurant), but that he was setting the standard by which she could measure her future dates. The goal for the evening was for Marie to aspire to high standards.

And that's what you want for your daughter. You don't want her to settle. You want her to want the best. Teach her that a guy who will treat her like a princess is definitely worth waiting for. And *she's* definitely worth the wait as well!

From time to time, Bill still has father-daughter dates with Marie. Whether it's a movie night, an evening at a fondue restaurant, or some other activity, it's his chance to simply treat his daughter like a princess and to remind her that she needs to keep her standards high.

When a father is able to fill his daughter's heart, she's not in a hurry to allow the first boy who looks her way to become her boyfriend.

THE GRANDFATHER IN HER LIFE

You may not have a husband. Perhaps you're divorced or your husband is deceased. You may be a single mom who wants the best for her daughter. Is there another male family member whom you can ask to spend some special time with her? Please use discernment in choosing a male role model for her. Don't ask just any male family member to do this; he needs to be someone you fully trust, and someone who shares your morals. Grandfathers can be great with this, because they were brought up in a day when it was simply expected for the male to open doors, let the woman walk first, etc.

Her grandfather may not live in the same city or state as you do, but they could still share an extremely special bond through e-mails, phone calls, and letters. You could even create a list of things you want to eventually be discussed between the two of them, and in his own time, through long-distance communication, he can bring these things up with your daughter.

ANOTHER MALE

My friend Sharla is a single mom with a sixteen-year-old daughter, Shayna. When Shayna asked for a True Love Waits ring (that ring I talked about earlier—it symbolizes a commitment to sexual purity until marriage), her mom wanted a significant male to present the ring to her daughter. So she called Shayna's favorite uncle, Jim. He wasn't really familiar with the True Love Waits concept, but Sharla explained the procedure to him: He'd take Shayna out to dinner, present to her the standard to remain sexually pure until marriage, and give her the ring.

Sharla didn't know if he'd go for it or not. He didn't have a teenager, and she didn't want it to be awkward for him. But he and Shayna had always shared a special bond, and he agreed to do it. Sharla was planning on purchasing the ring herself and giving it to Jim to present to Shayna, but Jim got so into it that he went to a jewelry store, picked out a ring, and presented it to Shayna during a special evening. She wears the ring proudly and says it has special meaning because her uncle cared enough about her to make a special night of it.

Maybe it's a brother, an uncle, or a special male friend in your church who's close to your family. But pray about finding a male who can help fill your daughter's heart. Ask God to direct you to the right person; He will.

If you're interested in purchasing purity jewelry with the words "True Love Waits" on it, the best place I've found is Factory 79 (*www.Factory79.com*). They produce an amazing variety of True Love Waits jewelry (necklaces, rings; gold, silver) at extremely affordable prices, and they provide a commitment card with every piece of purity jewelry. This way, the person who presents the girl with the jewelry has something to talk about while giving her the ring. The card describes the meaning of the commitment, and it has a place for the recipient to sign her name and date it.

Many girls wear their purity ring until their wedding night, when they present the ring to their husband. "I've worn this for _____ years as my commitment to God, my parents, myself, you, and my future children. Tonight I give you this symbol of my purity." The husband then keeps it in a special place, and in turn, he will present the same ring to their son or daughter during their teen years.

THE YOUTH LEADER IN HER LIFE

Maybe your daughter has a youth pastor, Sunday school teacher, or discipleship mentor in her life who can spend quality time with her on a regular basis. This doesn't have to be a male. Your daughter also needs older females who can speak truth into her heart. It's nice to have another female in her life she can look up to.

This woman can help fill your daughter's heart every time they go for a Coke, grab some coffee, get a hamburger, work out at the gym, or simply window-shop. The more secure you are in allowing other solid role models into your daughter's life, the more you'll see her heart being filled with precious love that won't have to come from a teen boy.

HEALTHY GIRLFRIENDS

Encourage good same-age female friendships for your daughter—without picking her friends for her. If your daughter is having trouble making friends, encourage her to get involved in things that will enable her to make friends: drama club, choir, track team, softball, debate, crafts, scrapbooking clubs, etc.

Let your house become the home everyone wants to come to. Encourage your daughter to have her friends over often! Rent a cotton candy machine or snow cone machine, make caramel apples, start a scrapbooking club, start a teen Bible study in your living room, have weekly movie nights, encourage her to start a book club that meets on your porch—anything to get kids inside your home.

Again, these are wonderful ways to fill your daughter's heart with fun and wholesome things so she won't look for a guy or something else to fill the void.

BE A DISCIPLER

You are a discipler to your daughter. Make sure you're filling her heart with the right perspectives, the right habits, the right lifestyle. How you live, think, and react to others is teaching her valuable lessons and filling her heart. How you love your husband is huge. Are you showing affection to him in front of her? Has she never seen you reach for his hand or give him a kiss? These are valuable lessons about love that you want to make sure get grounded in her heart.

Are you gossiping about others? Do you make fun of your husband?

Are you sarcastic about his weaknesses? Do you share your disappointments in your marriage with her? Again, these things *will* fill her heart. And if her heart isn't being filled with the right things, she's going to seek a guy, sarcasm, gossip, the Internet, etc., to fill the void.

Again, though you didn't ask for this role, *you* are her discipler. Your words and your actions will stay with her for a lifetime. What are you filling her heart with? And how are you filling it?

GAINING ACCESS TO HER HEART

Hal and Debbi Perkins, my youth pastors during my teen years, have successfully raised and discipled four grown children who are all currently in full-time ministry. Hal has written a book titled *If Jesus Were a Parent: Coaching Your Child to Follow Jesus.* The following excerpt describes how he moved inside his daughter's heart.

Many years of relating, meeting, and discipling preceded the following offer I made to [my daughter] Deborah. Deborah and I were out on our weekly appointment (my time to listen to her, to know her). It was 4:00 Wednesday afternoon. We were driving on one of Oklahoma City's straight, wide major thoroughfares. I was being "fatherish"—asking probing questions about what was going on. I could sense the stress—even irritation—in her heart by the way she was sitting, by the look on her face, and by the struggle we were having in communicating. The questions I was asking were about the young men who were taking great interest in her. The current one was a very popular guy; very good looking, first team all-city football player. It wouldn't take Einstein to observe that Deborah had suddenly blossomed into a very attractive young lady. For whatever reasons, she had not received nearly the favorable attention from her peers that her triplet siblings had as they grew up. To suddenly be the center of attention, especially from one of the "big men on campus," was heady stuff. I knew that Deborah's heart resolve was to follow Jesus. I was concerned that the pressures she would face from dating these guys would push her commitments to Jesus to the limit. I sensed that the attention she was getting was tantalizing and capturing her heart. Our heavenly Father effortlessly sees and knows the heart: attitudes, emotions, motives. Earthly parents must work hard to discover the heart.

When I attempted to "open her heart," it was very difficult for both Deborah and for me. I was not able to get the deepest issues out in the open for consideration. I understood that it was too "dangerous" for Deborah to expose what she was truly feeling—maybe thinking—probably wanting. If she did open up, I might not agree or approve. She wanted my approval. Worse yet, I might do what parents often do. I might try to separate her from this tantalizing, thrilling, new adventure she was delightfully experiencing. No matter how carefully I probed, it felt to me that she was dodging the core issues for which I was searching. For several weeks I had been trying to open her heart with respect to her male friend. No real progress.

I believe I was led by the Holy Spirit to make a bold move. I credit the Holy Spirit because, in retrospect, what was a very great "gamble" on my part resulted in her being saved from what appeared to be a very negative direction. Here is my best memory of what happened.

We stopped at one of her favorite eating places—Chili's—for one of her favorite nutritious meals—Diet Coke with lime and chips and salsa. I can see myself leaning across the table. I was about to make Deborah an offer. "I am very aware of the pressures you are facing with Joe [not his name]. I know you want me to be excited about your relationship with him. You can sense that I'm a little leery. I could forbid you to see him, and I know you would obey me—with your will." (For 15 years Deborah had been taught to obey. The one universal rule we had at our house was that if Mom or Dad gave a directive, it was to be obeyed. There were a few basic housekeeping rules, but we liked helping our kids think with Jesus about what He wanted in each unique situation. We were, therefore, willing to take many issues on a case-by-case study. But we had the final say. The kids had been taught and trained to submit to our authority.

Back to the date and my "dangerous offer.") "I know you would obey me with your will. But your thoughts about him, your feelings for him, and your desires regarding him would live on in your heart, for at least a while. If I directed you to break up, you may or may not be willing to share your heart with me. It seems like you are closing your heart to me now. At this point in your development, I believe I would be of the most help to you by being a friend with whom you can without fear freely share your desires and thoughts. I think that would be more helpful than retaining control over your external behavior as your 'dad.'"

It is important to restate that Deborah's willingness to submit to parental authority was firmly in place. It is very important for us, as children of God, to be committed to obeying God even when we don't understand and don't want to obey. God does some of His very best work in our hearts when we are obeying Him, in spite of what we think and want.

Several points were at stake. I want to raise just one. I wanted to be of the most help possible to Deborah. Because we had had a date almost every week for many years (plus our normal family life), I had a "feel" for her heart. I believed at this time in her development it would be best to make a gamble, an offer. So I did. "Deborah, I will make you an offer. It is based on my confidence in you that if you make a promise to me that you will keep it. Here's the offer: I will, from this moment on, never again tell you what you have to do, or cannot do. In exchange for this freedom, you must promise me that you will do your very best to be absolutely open with me about everything in your heart—what you feel, what you think, what you want, and why—and you will let me ask you anything. Further, you will carefully listen to my counsel and ask the Lord to show you if my input to your situation is best for you. If you take my counsel, I will support you in the consequence. If you ignore my counsel, I will love you and determine how much to help you when you experience the consequences of your choices."

This may seem like a dangerous position for a parent of a sophomore. I knew Deborah's good history with Jesus. I knew that soon she would be on her own—making big decisions based on her emotions, thoughts, desires—without her parents. I believed that if I had access to her heart, and she would seriously consider my response to her heart, I would have more influence on her future than if I controlled her behavior. I was willing to give up my positional authority to strengthen my relational and rational authority. I did it earlier than I had planned, but I was sensing this would be my best hope to help her. I believed I could disciple her far better by influencing her heart than by temporarily modifying her behavior with a rule but risk shutting her down and losing input to her heart.

Now a young adult, as Deborah recalls this time, she says,

"My dad extended my boundary lines and honored me and gave me dignity and freedom of choice which saved me from a thousand deaths. I know that if he would have come down on me and out of fear enclosed me any more than he did, then I would have made choices that would have hurt me far worse than giving me freedom and letting me make very significant choices on my own. There were still boundary lines, but they were extended. Because of that, I was able to make more decisions and learn. I ended up never rebelling. Just like in Psalm 18:35, 'Your gentleness has made me great.' (NLT) God allowed King David to come forth in voluntary love, which takes such great maturity and wisdom. My dad did that for me, and I think that is one of the greatest principles of making disciples. He showed me great mercy. His gentleness and the way he led me helped me through some deep waters. But it was not out of fear; it was out of his confidence in God's mercy. Therefore, he could be merciful with me. That was the greatest thing that he did in a very slippery time. . . . In a slippery time in my life, he gave me a greater boundary line. It is just the opposite of what a human should do. When something is slippery, you should increase the control and not give more freedom. But my dad gave more freedom in a time when I was in a slippery way and that saved my life. Of course, there were a lot of years of making progress up to this point, but in the teenage years, this is critical. If the parents have worked hard to keep relationship, they can be huge on mercy, on tenderness and gentleness. It is so important they don't operate out of fear, but out of confidence and mercy. They have to experience this from God or they won't be able to feel it for their children.

"They need to be like Jesus to their children. Every time that I went out with my dad, I was so aware of letting him know my heart and of trying to articulate the real depths of my heart so that we could stay friends even though I knew he didn't agree with the guy I was dating."

Was the decision good or bad? Parents can require rebellious teens to come in at midnight, but they cannot control their thoughts, emotions, and desires. If the heart is independent, rebellious, confused, angry, hostile, arrogant, etc., sooner or later bad choices with terrible consequences will occur.

(Used with permission from Hal Perkins. Copyright © 2006. For more information on this book, contact office@gvnaz.org; 509-882-1660.)

BOTTOM LINE

We're told in 1 Samuel 16:7 that though man looks at outward appearance, God looks at the heart. As you're striving to fill your daughter's heart, make an effort as well to truly see inside her heart. Get to know her heart. Why? Because her heart is where all her emotions and attitudes of life will be stored. Proverbs 4:23 says, "Above all else, guard your heart, for it is the wellspring of life."

Getting inside your daughter's heart is an honor, and it's also a process. Hold her heart carefully. When she shares with you, view it as someone placing gold, pearls, or precious jewels into your lap. You may not agree with what she shares; but you can learn to value her vulnerability.

If you don't agree with what she's sharing, gently ask pointed questions:

- "Why do you feel this way?"
- "Can you share with me what led you to this decision?"
- "How do you think Christ feels about this?"
- "How do you think I feel about it?"

- "Do you know—beyond all doubt—that I love you?" (Anytime you can, remind your daughter of your love for her in your conversations.)
- "If Christ were here in the flesh, how do you think He'd advise you?"
- "What does the Bible have to say about your situation?"
- "Would you be willing to spend some time in prayer and in the Bible, seeking God's will on this matter?"
- "Will you let me pray *with* you about this?"

As you bring Christ into discussions with your daughter, you have an opportunity to help her discover deceit, faulty thinking, and bad attitudes that may have taken residence inside her heart. As her mom, you want to be used of God to remove those unsightly areas and replace them with truth and purity.

It's up to you to fill your daughter's heart with things that are true, noble, right, pure, lovely, and admirable (Philippians 4:8). If *you* don't fill her heart, the world will!

MOM'S PAYCHECK

If a typical stay-at-home mom with two school-age children earned a paycheck, her annual salary would be:

National low: $64,374
National median: $116,805
National high: $174,061

—Mom.Salary.com

Chapter 8

THE TOP SEVEN ISSUES BETWEEN MOMS AND DAUGHTERS

You'll probably deal with a zillion different issues with your daughter during her growing-up years, but here are some of the most common issues you'll encounter.

NUMBER ONE: COMMUNICATION

I receive approximately twelve hundred letters and e-mails from teen girls around the world every month (and some from moms). My heart always grieves when there's a communication breakdown between the two that results in a strained relationship.

A teen girl writes, "I really want a tight relationship with my mom, but she's so busy. Spending time with me just doesn't seem to be a priority in her life."

And a mom writes, "I'd love to have a closer relationship with my daughter, but it seems as though her friends are her top priority. She's always on the go. I don't think she even wants me around."

Basically, mom and daughter are both wanting the same thing. Why aren't they achieving it? Simply because they're not communicating. Moms, if you want a closer relationship with your daughter, you need to initiate it. You're the adult; take the responsibility.

If she balks, keep at it. Remember, you're the adult; you're in charge. Make time for her. Be willing to rearrange your schedule. Your daughter may or may not be willing to rearrange hers at first, but if you set the example, she may follow suit.

I've planned and hosted two mother-daughter cruises, and I'm always touched by the comments that moms and daughters make on the evaluations:

- "I loved getting to laugh with my mom."
- "It was great having my mom all to myself."
- "I got to really have fun with my daughter instead of having to be the heavy. I didn't have to ask her about homework, chores, or responsibilities. We just had fun together."

And at our national mother-daughter conferences (*www.Closer MomsandDaughters.com*), I'm equally impressed with the comments at the end of the day:

- "I loved spending an entire day with my mom."
- "Thanks for giving me my daughter back."
- "My daughter hasn't told me in four years that she loves me. She's telling me now."
- "My mom and I prayed together. It was so cool."
- "I thought my daughter knew how much I loved her, but I realized today that I haven't told her that in a long time. I made sure she knows today, and I'm going to keep telling her."

- "I finally let my mom know about some secrets I'd been keeping from her."

It all boils down to communication. If you're a good communicator, your daughter will more than likely pick up on those skills and reflect your communication style. So think about it: How are you communicating? What are you communicating?

Many teen girls go through phases of not communicating with their moms. If this is happening, let me repeat: You're the adult. Take the initiative. Communicate plainly and simply that you need to hear her thoughts and her heart. Let her know that you want to know what she's feeling and experiencing.

If she still balks at the idea, I encourage you to try the journal approach. Purchase a new notebook to be shared between the two of you. Start a page with some fun and easy questions: "What's your favorite thing to do with our family?" "What's your favorite meal that I make?" Then give her the journal and ask her to anwer the questions and provide a list for you to answer. Eventually, deepen the questions you ask and the topics you discuss.

The bottom line? Most moms want to be close to their daughters. And most daughters want to be close to their moms. Genuine communication is the key that makes this desire become a reality!

NUMBER TWO: LISTENING

I can already guess what you're thinking: *I listen to my daughter; she just doesn't* think *I do!* Though listening is actually a key component of effective communication, I'm listing it separately, because it can really stand on its own.

As a mom, you have the incredible ability to multitask; that's what makes you so amazing! You can cook dinner, iron a shirt, put a load of clothes in the dryer, sew a hem, paint your nails, and listen to your daughter all at the same time. And though you really do hear every single word she says, in her mind you're not tuned in simply because you're consumed with other things.

A teen girl defines listening by having your full attention. She needs you to look her in her face, to lock eyes with her. She needs you to see how she uses her hands to express herself. She wants you to notice the words she chooses and the way she tilts her head and flips her hair during specific parts of her story. She needs you to stop everything else and focus completely on her.

That's listening.

Now, it may be that you'll have to explain to your daughter that this kind of listening can't happen at five-thirty in the evening, because you have to get dinner ready for the family and juggle several other things. You may need to say to her, "Honey, what you're saying to me is very important. I really can hear every word you're sharing. But I'd rather give you my full, undivided attention. So let's plan on my coming into your room right before you turn in. I'll sit on the edge of your bed, and we'll have our own private conversation. We'll talk as long as you want."

The problem with this can be a funny one. When she's ready to spill, you'll probably be ready for bed. Many teen girls come to life later at night, when you're exhausted from a full day and need to crash. But genuine communication—and listening is a key element of that—will require some sacrifices. Please be willing to go the extra mile. When it comes to truly hearing your daughter's heart, there's no price too high to pay.

NUMBER THREE: STRUGGLE FOR POWER

During her teen years, your daughter will more than likely push the boundaries you've set for her. If your daughter is strong-willed, this will be more of an issue. But desiring more freedom is a natural part of growing up for her. She's yearning to stretch her wings and fly, and ultimately, your goal is for her to do that. Just not yet.

Trust her unless there's a reason not to. You're the one who knows her emotional maturity better than anyone. If you feel it's appropriate to extend her curfew half an hour, do so. But if she breaks curfew, rein her back in.

Your daughter needs to know that you ultimately have the final word. I hope you're encouraging open dialogue between the two of you. Your daughter needs to know it's okay to disagree with you—as long as she does it in a gentle and respectful manner. But she also needs to submit to your final authority. The final power still belongs to the parents!

NUMBER FOUR: DRESS

Another struggle for power often shows up in how your daughter wants to dress. Unless what she's wearing—and how she's wearing it—could cause someone to stumble or put the name of Christ in a bad light, allow her some freedom to experiment with a variety of styles.

Black may not be your favorite color, but your daughter may desire to wear a lot of it. First strive to discover what the underlying reason is. Does she want to fit in with a specific group of teens who are also wearing black? If so, what's the lifestyle of these teens? Are they Goth? Are they rebellious? Is she wanting to wear black because she feels it makes her look slimmer?

You may not have two piercings in your ears, but your daughter may ask permission to do so. Again, discuss the reasons she wants another piercing in her ear, and if it's something that's not going to harm her or her witness, consider letting her do it.

Your daughter may feel more at home in a baseball cap and pair of jeans than in slacks and a sweater or a dress. Again, choose your battles wisely! You want to save your no's for something that really matters . . . like modesty.

Also included here is how she dresses for specific occasions. You may experience a power struggle if you feel something requires a semiformal appearance and she doesn't. When I was growing up, most women wore dresses to church. Our youth group met on Wednesday evenings, and it was much more casual. Most everyone was in jeans or slacks. As much as I tried to convince my mom it was appropriate, she just couldn't consider allowing me to wear pants to church! So I had to keep wearing a dress or a skirt even on Wednesdays.

We battled over that one a long time, but she wouldn't budge. Because I loved my parents, and because of my relationship with Christ, I knew an issue of obedience was at stake. I obeyed, but I wasn't happy about it!

Today, many churches offer a more relaxed atmosphere. They simply want people there, regardless of what they're wearing. So this may never be an issue with you. But let's say your church has a banquet, and you think your daughter should be in a dress. All her friends, however, will be wearing pants. Because it's not a moral issue, I encourage you to allow her the freedom of blending in with friends from church.

NUMBER FIVE: MODESTY

This is one of the biggest issues that moms and daughters battle. It probably won't be settled in one discussion, but consider setting aside a good amount of time with your daughter to explain how her lack of modesty can affect the guys around her.

Whenever I address a group of teen girls on this matter, I'm first met with resistance:

- "It's not our fault guys are weird."
- "I shouldn't have to modify what I want to wear just so the guy next to me won't lust."
- "If a guy lusts after me, that's *his* problem."

Most teen girls just don't understand that guys are wired completely differently than girls. Help your daughter understand that a Christian young lady's first desire should be to please her heavenly Father. Explain that dressing in a godly manner is a responsibility that needs to be taken seriously by all Christians—guys *and* girls.

Underneath the umbrella of desiring to please God should be the desire to reflect Him in everything she does: dress, entertainment choices, how she talks, what she's involved in, etc. As Christian women, we want to help our Christian brothers grow stronger in the Lord. Why would we want to dress in a way that will tempt them or cause them to stumble?

It is our responsibility as Christian women to dress in a way that won't cause guys to be distracted or to have lustful thoughts. I wish girls could read the letters I receive from teen guys. Josh says, "It sure is hard to keep my mind on worship at youth group when the girl in front of me lifts her hands during a praise chorus and I can see half her back and how low her jeans are riding."

Dylan says, "I love it when I see a girl dressed modestly. It's like I can breathe a huge sigh of relief."

And Brady says, "When I see a girl wearing something too tight, too low, too short, and too revealing, I can't help but think she's desperate to get a message out—and it's not a message a Christian guy like me needs to hear."

Justin is grateful for the Christian girls in his youth group who *are* rising to the modesty challenge. "They have no idea how much they're helping us guys stay pure in our thought life when they walk into church wearing something that's modest. It really does help keep me focused on what our youth pastor is saying instead of trying to rein in my thoughts going wild with seeing a girl's tummy."

We need to teach our teen girls that this is simply how guys were created. All guys—Christian or not—are visual beings. Many girls think, "Not my boyfriend; he's a Christian. His thoughts would never go that direction."

While a Christian guy has a responsibility (with the help of the Holy Spirit) to rein his thoughts back in, it's only natural for his thoughts to go in a direction they shouldn't when he sees too much flesh.

So be willing to discuss tank tops, spaghetti straps, low-riders, etc. Help your daughter understand that modesty doesn't mean dressing like a prude. Teach her how to be stylish and modest at the same time.

NUMBER SIX: THE INTERNET

Music, movies, cell phones, and the Internet are as much a part of a teen girl's life as breathing. So it's obvious this area will become an issue for the two of you.

Most girls don't realize the incredible danger that's on the Internet. Many give out their hometown, the name of their school, and other personal bits of information about themselves without thinking twice. "I don't give out my address," they may say, "so I don't think it's any big deal."

Yet a skilled predator can trace a teen girl in her environment without much detail at all. I'll never forget a story in the news a few years ago. A teen girl was desperate to find a boyfriend, so she got in a chat room and was immediately smitten with a "teen guy" who said all the right things.

They continued to correspond, and their conversation escalated to the point where they decided to meet. She agreed to show up at a specific hotel in a city near her hometown. He gave her the room number and told her he'd be waiting for her inside.

Imagine the heartbreak when she entered the room to find her own father! He, too, had been looking for an encounter, and neither had any idea that they were actually corresponding with each other.

Does this mean you shouldn't allow your daughter to be on

MySpace or Facebook or any other social networking site? Again, you know her emotional maturity better than anyone. I know some teen girls who actually use these sites as a witnessing tool. But they're teens who are extremely grounded in their faith, smart about what they post, and extremely guarded in giving out any personal information regarding their surroundings.

If you feel okay about allowing your daughter to create a MySpace page or something similar, get involved *with* her on this project. Know at all times what she's posting and what others are putting on her site. I know many moms who have their own Facebook accounts just so they can be in the loop with what their daughters and friends are doing. I think that's great!

NUMBER SEVEN: ENTERTAINMENT CHOICES

When it comes to movies, strive to help your daughter learn to discern. If you can teach her how to do this, it will guide her in making wise choices for a lifetime. Instead of simply saying no, pull up a review of the movie in question. Discuss the review with her. How many times is God's name taken in vain? How much violence is in the movie? What's the premise? Is there sexual activity? Is this something that will draw her closer to her heavenly Father? Is this something that will distance her in her relationship with Christ?

An incredible resource is *PluggedInOnline.com*, a site produced by Focus on the Family, which covers the latest in youth trends, including movies, television shows, books, and music. They have tons of archived material on their Web site. Before seeing a movie, it would be wise to go to their site to read their review, and then discuss it with your daughter. Again, the goal is for her to learn to discern for herself.

Here's a fun example of a dad trying to teach his teen daughter about making wise entertainment decisions.

SPECIAL BROWNIES

Brooke asked permission to attend a PG-13 movie with some of her friends from school. It starred her favorite actor, and people from her church had even seen it and said it was great. Her dad listened to all her reasons for going and then asked, "Why do you think it has the 13 rating on it?"

"Well," Brooke admitted, "there is a scene where a building and several people are blown up, but the violence isn't too bad. And there are a few other minor things, but the special effects are incredible!"

Brooke's dad wouldn't give in. He simply said, "No."

A little later that same evening, he asked Brooke if she'd like some warm brownies he'd baked. He explained that he'd used the family's favorite recipe and added a little something new.

"What is it?" Brooke asked.

Her dad calmly replied that he'd added dog poop. "But it was only a little bit," he quickly added. "All the other ingredients are gourmet quality. I'm sure they'll be fantastic!"

"You're kidding, right?" Brooke asked in shock.

"No. Go ahead and try one."

Brooke wouldn't go near the brownies. Her dad acted surprised. "You'll hardly notice that one ingredient, Brooke," he said. But his daughter held firm and wouldn't give in.

Her dad then explained the meaning behind his charade. "The movie you want to see is just like these brownies. Your mind is telling you that a little bit of evil won't matter. But the truth is, even a little bit of poop makes the difference between a great treat and something disgusting and totally unacceptable."

Brooke was silent as her dad continued his explanation. "Brooke, even though the movie industry wants you to believe that most of today's movies are acceptable for adults and teens, the truth is they're not."

Now the truth is, we live in a sinful world. It's pretty hard to do anything—spend time with non-Christian friends or go out to eat—without confronting some wrong things. This story doesn't mean you should lock yourself in your bedroom and never come out! But it does mean that you need to make wise choices. You may not be able to avoid some wrong things, like being around people at school or work who take God's name in vain. But you can make careful choices to limit the amount of time you're exposed to stuff that will hurt you.[5]

Satan will work through movies, TV, music, and maybe even your friends to try and convince you that something questionable is really okay. Don't fall for his lies. He's the father of deceit. Keep your spiritual guard up and let the Holy Spirit guide your decisions.

---

[5] Excerpted from *The One Year Devos for Teens* by Susie Shellenberger. Tyndale House. Copyright © 2002. Used by permission.

Chapter 9

SEVEN SIGNS YOU'RE HEADED IN THE RIGHT DIRECTION

If you're doing a good job with your daughter, you want to know, right? And if you need improvement, you'll be able to discern from these signposts where your areas of weakness are.

NUMBER ONE: YOU'RE NOT IN COMPETITION WITH EACH OTHER

I'm not talking about a fun game of Ping-Pong! Your daughter feels the freedom to express herself within her own unique God-given gifts. They may be completely different from yours, but she doesn't feel she needs to measure up and become a great seamstress because you are. She feels free to be herself around her friends and feels confident in her relationship with you.

Roxanne often encouraged her daughter, Carissa, to invite friends to the house. But Carissa noticed that whenever her friends were over, her mom dressed and acted differently. Without realizing it, Roxanne was competing for attention from her daughter's friends.

When Carissa quit having friends over, her mom wanted to know why. "You're different when they're here, Mom," she said. "You dress like a teenager and try to talk hip. And you do stuff to try to be the center of attention. It makes me feel weird."

That was difficult for Roxanne to hear, but because Carissa had talked in a respectful way, and because they had a good relationship, she listened to her daughter and evaluated what she said. Roxanne realized Carissa was right. During her teen years, Roxanne's family had moved a lot, and she never had a lot of close friends. She realized she was trying to gain an experience she still yearned for.

Roxanne changed her behavior and apologized to her daughter. Carissa is back to having friends over, and Roxanne is careful to greet everyone and pop in on them every now and then in appropriate ways, but she generally stays out of the way. She has also joined a neighborhood craft club to cultivate some close friendships with other women.

Kaylee's friends loved hanging out at her house. Her mom always had fresh brownies or cookies and made each friend feel loved and welcomed in her home. She offered a safe haven for her daughter and friends without being overly involved in everything they were doing.

Kaylee had to get her mom's approval for the DVD she selected to show, and her mom simply popped into the room every now and then to ask if anyone needed something. She'd bring a pitcher of lemonade in with her, or another plate of brownies, but it was really her way of simply checking on everyone and making sure things were meeting a high standard.

If you and your daughter are in direct competition with each other, this is a sign of dysfunction. And again, I'm not talking about healthy competition in a game of tennis. Some moms and daughters compete for the attention of the man of the house. Others compete in diets and weight loss. These kinds of competitive actions only harm you and your daughter.

NUMBER TWO: YOU HAVE ACTIVITIES YOU DO TOGETHER

You may have to work hard to find something you can physically do with your daughter—especially if the two of you are opposites. She may like roller coasters, and you may enjoy the merry-go-round. She may like a fast-paced game of racquetball, and you may enjoy miniature golf. But find *something* the two of you can laugh about and do together.

Maybe it's go-carting, test-driving new cars off the lot, walking through the mall while eating a big cookie and counting all the bald men you see, photography, dancing, organizing an annual family garage sale, making ceramics and pottery, antiquing, starting a collection together, riding horses, baking, or taking a twice-annual road trip for just the two of you. Again, this may take some effort on your part, but it's worth it to laugh with your daughter and bond through a shared interest.

Shelby and Marissa go geocaching together. Annette and Sydney bake bread and deliver it to people who have been sick and missed church. Pam and Jessica love to shop at Goodwill. Alisha and Mia enjoy card-making.

And while you're doing things together, make sure your daughter sees you laugh at yourself. When you do something klutzy, instead of berating yourself, laugh it off. Allow her the fun of laughing with you during these moments.

Also, be willing to provide an environment that's conducive to laughter. My friend Suzi allows her high-school daughter, Heather, to invite as many friends as she wants to their home for an annual "Slop Night."

"The goal is simply to provide a fun atmosphere with my daughter and watch her go crazy with her friends," Suzi says. "We have it on a Saturday afternoon, and kids can stay as long as they want. I serve spaghetti, but everyone has to eat with his or her hands. We have Jell-O (again, eating with hands) and a few other fun things. But the highlight is the mud bowl in the backyard. We prepare a large muddy area ahead of time, and after lunch everyone plays flag football in the mud pit. It's hilarious and always provides lots of laughs."

NUMBER THREE: YOUR SELF-IMAGE ISN'T DETERMINED BY HER

She has the freedom to fail and learn from her own mistakes and knows that you love her unequivocally. Your identity isn't wrapped up in your daughter; it's based on an intimate, growing relationship with your heavenly Father.

When Nikki became pregnant outside of marriage, her mom's self-esteem plummeted. "I couldn't believe it," Joyce says. "She was involved in church, and we had set high standards for her. My world fell apart."

Joyce blamed herself, and that blame was evident to Nikki. "I suddenly felt as though my mom's life was completely destroyed because of me. She was embarrassed around her friends at church, and she kept asking me where she'd failed. Hey, it was my mistake, not hers! But I felt as though I was not only responsible to get myself together spiritually again, but that I would also have to figure out how to help *her* feel good about herself once more."

If your daughter feels your view of yourself is dependent on her, she'll never have the freedom to become all God desires for her. She can't be responsible for you. Your self-worth can be enhanced through your daughter, but it can't be based on her.

NUMBER FOUR: YOU HAVE SPIRITUAL DISCUSSIONS AND PRAY WITH EACH OTHER

As I stated at the beginning of the book, your greatest responsibility as a mom is to disciple your daughter. Are you able to teach her about God's Word? If not, get there!

Do whatever it takes to make God a reality in her life. Initiate spiritual discussions with her often. Talk about the sermon in church last week. Ask her what she's learning in youth group. Read and discuss the Bible together. And don't simply pray *for* her; determine to pray *with* her. (I realize this is a repeat of some ground we've already covered, but it's so vitally important, I just have to stress it again.) The most important conversations you'll have with your daughter will be the spiritual ones, because they're the ones that affect eternity.

NUMBER FIVE: YOUR DAUGHTER CAN TALK ABOUT GUYS WITHOUT FEAR OF JUDGMENT OR CONDEMNATION

Lynda wanted her daughter, Zoe, to know that nothing was off limits when it came to discussions between them. She told Zoe from the time she was a toddler that she could always ask Mom anything. Of course, as Zoe matured, her questions changed from, "Why is blue, blue?" to "What's a French kiss?" And as the questions matured, Lynda never expressed shock or irritation with her daughter.

"I was sometimes tempted to say, 'Where did you hear that word?' or 'We don't use that phrase,' " Lynda says. "But I realized she was asking me out of innocence, and I had the unique opportunity to shape her values as I answered her questions."

When Zoe got old enough to date, her questions reflected what she'd heard from other girls in the lunchroom or on the softball field. "What does it mean when a girl says she let a guy go to second base with her?" And "I heard someone talk about cybersex. What is that?"

Lynda adds, "I was actually grateful she was coming to me with her questions instead of getting her answers from people who didn't share my values or my faith."

Though Zoe's questions and openness about guys sometimes scared Lynda, she never showed fear or disappointment in her face. She continued to welcome her daughter's conversations about the opposite sex and used their dialogue to shape her value system.

NUMBER SIX: SHE HAS ONE OR MORE HEALTHY MALE RELATIONSHIPS

Christy always had a boyfriend during her teen years, so when her daughter entered middle school, she talked about it a lot with her daughter, Amber. Without realizing it, Christy was placing too high a priority on her daughter's having a boyfriend. Whenever the school had an activity—football game, dance, fall festival—she'd pressure Amber about asking a boy to go with her.

In doing this, Christy gave her daughter the idea that it was really up to her to make a relationship happen instead of trusting God in His perfect timing to work out the relationships in her life.

We'll fast-forward this story, and you can probably guess how Amber turned out. If she wasn't dating someone, she felt worthless. She had to have a guy by her side, and when she didn't, she fell into a state of depression. Christy, unfortunately, didn't know how to teach Amber how to develop healthy male relationships.

Don't push your daughter into romantic relationships. Trust God in this important area of her life. But encourage her to have male friends as well as female friends. Making friends with guys during her teen years not only is normal but teaches her how to interact socially with the opposite sex.

And, of course, having healthy male relationships in her life doesn't simply mean guy friends her age. It also means a healthy relationship with adult males. How does she interact with her dad? With her male teachers at school? Helping your daughter view males in a healthy way is a sure sign you're headed in the right direction with her.

NUMBER SEVEN: YOU CAN EACH SAY "I LOVE YOU" AND KNOW THE OTHER TRULY MEANS IT

Hopefully you're telling your daughter every single day that you love her. Are you showing her as well? Those three precious words have to be backed by action for her to know you mean it. Check out 1 John 3:18: "Let us stop just *saying* we love people; let us *really* love them, and *show* it by our *actions*" (TLB).

If the apostle John places this much emphasis on loving others, how much more so should we be showing our daughters how much we love them? Put action to your words.

Place a sticky note on her bathroom mirror expressing your love. Pack a note in her lunch that says, "Just because we're not together right now doesn't mean I'm not thinking of you."

Or make a card and put it on her pillow: "I can't even articulate how much I love you!" Or scribble a note with crayons on construction paper: "You mean the world to me." How about writing on a page inside her notebook? "Do you know that you're one of the very most important people in the entire world to me?"

Being able to say "I love you" and hear your daughter say it back to you, knowing that she means it, is what will keep the two of you close during times of disagreement and strained communication.

A MOTHER'S JOB DESCRIPTION
FROM A TO Z

Affirmer	*Nutrition Genius*
Baker	*Office Clerk*
Carpooler	*Potty Trainer*
Driving Instructor	*Q-Tip Professional*
Engineer	*Rescuer*
Fireproofer	*Specialist in Everything*
Groomer	*Teacher*
Health-Care Administrator	*Ultimate Comforter*
Icky Stuff Eliminator	*Values Coach*
Jungle Gym Assembler	*Wound Fixer*
Kitchen Pro	*X-Ray Vision Expert*
Locater of All Things Lost	*Yo-Yo Instructor*
Monster Slayer	*Zookeeper*

Chapter 10

THE DAUGHTER WHO'S LOST

You may be reading this book with a broken heart because you have a daughter who has rebelled, run away, or refused to accept Christ as her Savior. You may have done everything right—you prayed, you affirmed, you guided—but she's still lost. Take heart and remember that God has a special promise for you: "Train a child in the way he should go, and when he is old he will not turn from it" (Proverbs 22:6).

Hopefully you'll get to see your daughter return to you and surrender to Christ, but it could be that this may not happen during your lifetime. But have faith that God is trustworthy, and He wants your daughter on the right track even more than you do!

It's difficult to imagine anyone could love your daughter more than you do, but God does! Though you love your daughter immensely, you're only loving with the limited capacity of a human. God loves her supernaturally, and He's willing to move heaven and earth to get her where she needs to be spiritually.

GOD ANSWERS PRAYER!

Your prayers make a difference! Remember the Old Testament king Hezekiah? He became deathly ill, and the prophet Isaiah told him he wouldn't recover from this illness. When the king heard this news, he pleaded with the Lord to extend his life. God not only heard his prayer, He answered it by giving him fifteen more years (see 2 Kings 20:1–6).

And when Joshua was in the thick of battle and needed more sunlight to win the war, He prayed that God would extend the day and keep the sun from moving. Take a peek at what God did: "The sun stopped in the middle of the sky and delayed going down about a full day. There has never been a day like it before or since" (Joshua 10:13–14).

God answers prayer!

He doesn't always answer the way we want Him to, but He always answers. And His timing is often completely different from ours, but His timing is perfect. When we think He's being slow, He's actually right on time. Check out my favorite verse regarding God's timing and answered prayer: "But these things I plan won't happen right away. Slowly, steadily, surely, the time approaches when the vision will be fulfilled. If it seems slow, do not despair, for these things will surely come to pass. Just be patient! They will not be overdue a single day!" (Habakkuk 2:3 TLB).

The overriding truth I get from that Scripture is that God is never late! He's always on time. It's just that His timing and our timing usually aren't the same. If you're committed to fully trusting the Lord, that means continuing to trust Him even when things aren't working out the way you wanted and even when your specific situation seems totally out of control.

REMEMBER THE PRODIGAL?

You may be familiar with the New Testament story of the prodigal son. He rebelled against authority and demanded that his father give him the inheritance that was his. Dad handed over the money, and the son split.

He lived a lifestyle opposite from the one he was brought up in. The Bible tells us he wasted his money on women and drink. Your daughter may be in a similar situation. Perhaps she has established a lifestyle that's contrary to how you raised her. Even though she knows better, she's doing drugs, is sexually involved, and is partying like there's no tomorrow. What can you do?

Do what the father of the prodigal son did: pray, hope, and wait.

PRAY

Let me remind you that God hears every single one of your prayers! When you pray, He's all ears. As a Christian, you have a direct prayer line straight into the throne room of heaven. God's line is never busy, He doesn't use caller ID to screen calls, and you're never forwarded. When you pray, He knows it's you, He understands your situation, and He loves listening to your heart.

Did you know there will come a time when God will silence all of heaven simply to focus on prayer? That's how important the prayers of His children are!

> When the Lamb had broken the seventh seal, there was silence throughout all heaven for what seemed like half an hour.
>
> Revelation 8:1 TLB

The apostle John is writing the last book of the Bible—Revelation—and much of this book deals with future events. He's not making anything up; he's writing exactly what the angel of the Lord tells him to (see Revelation 1:1–2). So this thirty-minute silence isn't fiction; it's something that will actually happen someday.

It hasn't occurred yet, but there will come a time—during the great tribulation—when those who have accepted Christ as Savior will be in the midst of the heaviest persecution known to mankind. In desperation, they'll lift their voices to heaven asking, "How long, O Lord? How much longer?"

And Scripture shows us that God will be so intent and so focused on their prayers that He will literally silence the entire kingdom of heaven. Do you realize what this means?

The angels who are constantly doing His bidding will be quiet. The twenty-four elders surrounding the throne in praise and worship will be stilled. The saints from ages past will hush. *All of heaven will be completely silenced for about half an hour.*

It's as though God is saying, "Ssssshhhhh! They're praying, and there's nothing more important to me than what they're saying. Everyone and everything in my entire kingdom must cease to make noise. My children are praying!"

Wow. Does that help you realize how much attention God pays to the prayers offered to Him? When you pour out your heart to God, I can almost hear Him saying, "I'm all over it! I hear you. I understand."

Never quit praying for your daughter!

HOPE

No matter how impossible the situation with your daughter becomes, do *not* lose hope. Why? Because anything is possible with God. You don't serve a God of maybe. You serve a God of promise. A Father of dependability. A Savior of faithfulness.

The prodigal son's father didn't give up hope. Though the situation *seemed* hopeless, he continued to pray and hope. I can see him each morning standing in his driveway, squinting his eyes and looking as far as he can see, *hoping* that today will be the day his son returns.

When Staci entered college, she decided she'd had enough of church. Though she was very involved throughout her teen years, she was now on her own and wanted to try things her way.

"It broke my heart," Karen says. "My daughter loved youth group, she participated in mission trips, she invited friends from school to church, and she was extremely vocal about her faith. I couldn't understand the sudden change."

But Karen and her husband continued to pray for Staci. They didn't know that during her high school years Staci was date raped and never dealt with it. They didn't know she had tried alcohol because she felt pressured to do so one night at a party and couldn't forgive herself.

So feeling ashamed and guilt-ridden, Staci walked away from her faith when she went to college. "She did everything that could possibly break our hearts," Karen says. "At one point she thought she had a sexually transmitted infection and was scared beyond words. I took her to get tested. Fortunately she didn't have an STI, but she continued to drink and hang out with all the wrong people."

Karen maintained open communication with her daughter. "I wanted to lecture her; I wanted to scream; I wanted to force her to come home. But I knew none of those things would work with her. So I simply continued to love her and hope that God would bring her back."

Staci was open with her mom. They communicated often, though it wasn't about things Karen wanted to hear. Staci was honest about her lifestyle, and Karen continued to let her daughter know that she was praying for her and that she loved her unconditionally.

A few years passed and Staci got pregnant. She decided to marry the father of her child, but things didn't get better. "Though things kept looking worse and worse," Karen says, "I just kept praying and hoping. I tried to rest in the fact that I was doing all I could do and God would have to do the rest."

One Sunday Staci, her husband, and the baby came to church. Though Staci had heard the same message over and over for years, something about it took hold in her heart. She felt the tug of the Holy Spirit on her life, and she recommitted herself to God.

A few weeks later, her husband gave his life to God, and shortly afterward, they asked the pastor to dedicate their baby to His glory. Staci and her husband are now extremely involved in church, and Karen gives her heavenly Father the credit for answering prayer and keeping her hope alive.

Your story may not end like Karen's, but there is hope. As long as you continue to pray for your daughter, there *is* hope!

WAIT

Probably even harder than hoping is waiting. I'm naturally an impatient person. I want it fast, and I want it now. I was thrilled when Minute Rice became microwavable! Hey, it only took a minute before, but now it's even faster because I can nuke it in the microwave! I just love fast. I think fast, talk fast, walk fast, and am fast. So when it comes to waiting, I have a really hard time.

Waiting is even tougher when it involves someone we love. But the Creator of the universe waited on you, and He can provide the strength and endurance you need to wait on your daughter.

Pam's daughter never talked much about God. "We attended church as a family," Pam says. "And we prayed together at meals, but I never was really sure where Trista stood with God. I should have been more straightforward with her, but I became a Christian later in life, and I missed a lot of those special opportunities to pray with her before soccer games or read the Bible with her."

Trista was obedient to her parents and wasn't rebellious, but she just wasn't vocal about faith at all. "My husband and I talked about our own faith in front of her, and we'd direct the conversation toward her, but she'd never give us a response that indicated she was a Christian."

Pam prayed and fasted often for her daughter—and simply kept waiting. "During spring break of her junior year in college, Trista came home," Pam remembers. "It was so good to have her back. We shopped together, laughed together, and even shared a few tears, but there still was no change in her willingness to discuss spiritual matters."

Pam kept loving and continued to wait. "It was her last night at home before she was to return to college," Pam remembers. "It was a little after midnight. I'd been in bed for a couple of hours already, but I got up to get a drink from the kitchen and noticed her bedroom light was on. I stepped inside her room and saw her on the bed with her Bible. It wasn't open, but she was holding it in her lap. 'I'm ready,' she said. 'I'm finally ready to pray with you.'

"I could have shouted from the roof, but of course I didn't," Pam says. "I simply sat on the edge of her bed and asked if she wanted to give her heart to Christ."

Trista confirmed that she wanted to become a Christian. "I know you've been waiting a long time," she told her mom. "But I just wasn't ready. It's not that I was sowing wild oats or anything; I just wanted to think everything through. I'm ready now. Thanks for being patient, Mom."

Can you imagine the prodigal son's dad when his wait was finally rewarded? That's when the party began! And you too will feel like celebrating when God brings your daughter home. Don't give up. Don't stop praying. Keep hoping, and continue to wait. The God who promised, "Train a child in the way he should go, and when he is old he will not turn from it," is faithful. He keeps His promises. He *will* do what He says!

HE KNOWS!

One of the Old Testament names for God is *El Roi*. It means "the God who knows." Take comfort in the fact that He knows all about your daughter. My friend Lisa has a daughter in college who's not walking with the Lord right now. "I get such comfort," she says, "in knowing that He knows all about Riley and everything she's going through."

Lisa clings to Psalm 139. It tells us that God knows every detail of our lives—even when we sit and stand. "God knows what's going to come out of Riley's mouth before she even utters one word," Lisa says. "When I'm frightened because I have no idea where my daughter is or what she's doing, He reminds me that He knows exactly what she's up to. He knows the people she's with, what she's drinking, what she's thinking. He knows it all. As her mom, I can't know all that, but as a child of the King, I can rest in His provision that He knows and cares."

Lisa asks the Lord to let her know what she needs to know about Riley. "I wish I could be with her 24-7," Lisa says. "But that's impossible. She's away at college, and I have other children who need my attention. But I'm trusting that when I need to know something about her, God will tell me."

And He does! God sometimes wakes Lisa in the middle of the night and directs her to pray in a specific manner for Riley. Or during the middle of the day as Lisa involves herself in a career and her family, God will often stop her with something very specific to pray regarding her daughter.

As Lisa prays for her daughter, she often prays Scripture and inserts her own name or her daughter's name. "I especially love Psalm 139," she says. "I love praying the whole chapter, but the last part has special meaning for me: 'Search Riley, O God, and know her heart; test her thoughts. Point out anything you find in Riley that makes you sad, and lead her along the path of everlasting life.' "

HIS PERSPECTIVE

It's important to recognize that what you may consider an emergency isn't always an emergency in God's eyes. He's not surprised by anything your daughter is doing right now. Nothing leaves Him at a loss for words. He has never wrung His hands and paced heaven, worried about how He can intervene and help your daughter. Again, He knows all. And though things may seem completely out of control from your perspective, you're not seeing it from His eyes.

God has a million and one ways to reach your daughter. His resources are unlimited, and He's willing to use every single one of them to bring her back to Him if necessary. "So often I want to launch into a Sunday school lesson when I'm talking with Riley," Lisa says. "But I know her, and I know she'd shut me out. She'd get quiet and simply start distancing herself from me. I have to learn to be silent at times and just let God work through the variety of ways that He wants to move in her life."

PETITIONING GOD

Lisa and her husband continue to petition their heavenly Father on Riley's behalf. They'll keep praying, hoping, and waiting. And as they pray, they ask God to bless them with His wisdom and discernment. "The Bible tells us that when we don't know what or how to pray, the Holy Spirit will intervene and take our prayers to God," she says.

So, Mom, when you can't even find the words to pray, the Holy Spirit is in essence approaching Christ on the throne and saying, "She's here. Your daughter is in your presence, and her heart is so burdened for her own daughter that she can't find the words to express herself. She's crying, Father. She's moaning. She has lost all strength, but she comes to you in faith to intercede for her precious lost one." And the Holy Spirit will continue to tell the Lord what you can't even begin to express.

"We also want to continue to ask for His guidance in finding a healthy balance between helping Riley and enabling her," Lisa says. "I want her to know we're here for her and that we will always love her unconditionally, but we can't allow ourselves to enable her. Sometimes that line is so fine that it's hard to discern. We have to rely on the Lord to help us know the difference."

As you continue to petition God on behalf of your daughter, ask Him to bring her to godly sorrow when she encounters difficulties. Godly sorrow is different from worldly sorrow. A worldly sorry expresses itself with "Why me? How come I have all these problems? No one cares about me or understands."

A godly sorrow, however, leads to repentance. King David, when confronted by the prophet Nathan regarding David's sin of adultery with Bathsheba, felt godly sorrow. He was truly remorseful that he had disobeyed God. Godly sorrow leads to repentance, and God will always forgive a genuinely repentant heart.

NO MAGIC BULLET

Wouldn't it be great if there were a "spiritual vitamin" you could actually give to your wayward daughter? She'd take the vitamin, and within a few hours she'd surrender her life to the lordship of Christ. Wow! If it were possible to create such an item, someone would probably be a billionaire.

Unfortunately, there is no magic formula, vitamin, or bullet that will guarantee your daughter will come to Christ, come back to Christ, or remain close to Christ. She will blow it—just as you will—because like you, she's human. Please be encouraged, Mom, that a mistake isn't going to send your daughter down the path of destruction. You need to allow her the space to make mistakes. The important thing is not keeping your daughter from making mistakes. The real issue is how she recovers and moves on from her mistakes. That's where you come in.

Keep praying!

Continue hoping!

Persist in waiting!

You serve a God of faithfulness, and He will keep His Word!

JANE OF ALL TRADES

The job titles that best matched a mom's definition of her work (in order of hours spent per week):

housekeeper

day-care center teacher

cook

computer operator

laundry machine operator

janitor

facilities manager

van driver

CEO

psychologist

—Salary.com

Chapter 11

MOM: A SPIRITUAL HERO

I was hosting a mother-daughter cruise, and we were having an absolute blast! We had chartered the entire ship, which meant we had creative control over everything. We were able to shut down the casinos, remove the alcohol, and select the music that was played in the hallways and around the pool. We were even allowed to create our own programming on one channel on the television inside the cabins.

It was heaven on earth. More than fourteen hundred moms and daughters laughing, swimming, shopping, praying, and growing spiritually together. As cruise host, I was also one of the main speakers. After one particular session, Shirley grabbed me and asked if we could have lunch together. "Susie, I'm here with my thirteen-year-old daughter, Jacquelyn," she said. "After hearing you speak last night, we went back to the cabin and Jacquelyn just stared at me. I asked her what she was thinking, and she said she'd never heard anything like that before. She didn't know God could be exciting."

Shirley went on to tell me that although they attended church, it was boring and there was no youth program. "*I* don't even get anything out of the sermons," she said. "I'm now beginning to see how my children have missed out on spiritual stuff that I've taken for granted."

I asked her to explain. "Well, *I* know God can be exciting," she said, "but my kids have never experienced that excitement. We don't have any kind of family devotions, and I'm just now beginning to realize that Jacquelyn doesn't really know the basics of Christianity."

I asked Shirley if she'd consider talking with her husband about seeking God's direction regarding the church they attend. She was definite. "I don't even have to think about it," she said. "When I get off this cruise, I'm telling him we've got to get to a church that has a youth program and can disciple our kids. And he and I need to get into a Bible study too. We've skimped by too long by simply walking in, sitting down, wading through a sermon, and walking out. That's the extent of our church involvement. I want my kids excited about God. And I want to get the spiritual excitement back that I used to have!"

I watched Shirley and Jacquelyn through the rest of the cruise. They were literally on the edge of their seats, soaking up the message of each speaker, each music artist, and each Christian entertainer.

After the cruise Shirley sent me an e-mail asking if I knew of a way she and her daughter could study the Bible together. I explained that I'd written a series of Bible study books for teen girls that could easily be done together and sent her the entire set.

Imagine my excitement when after only three weeks, Shirley e-mailed me again saying that they'd finished the first book and were diving into the second one. "I can't believe Jacquelyn's thirst for this stuff," she said. "I don't even have to remind her. She's sitting on her bed eating this stuff up! My husband wants me to ask if you have anything he and our son can do together. They're jealous of how Jacquelyn and I are growing!"

Ha! When a teen girl gets excited about God, nothing can stop her! And as Shirley prays with Jacquelyn and they study the Word together, Shirley is becoming her daughter's spiritual hero.

THE RIGHT TO GROW SPIRITUALLY

A teenager doesn't have a lot of rights. She doesn't have the right to vote, the right to drink, or the right to drive before sixteen. But she *does* have the right to own a relationship with God! Would you be willing to help your daughter with this right?

As mentioned earlier, I was brought up in a Christian home. Both of my parents and my brother were Christians. I mentioned how my dad would often gather the family together for prayer time. But I also want to mention how I often "caught" my mom praying and reading her Bible.

It wasn't unusual to walk into the kitchen and see Mom sitting at the table reading her Bible. It wasn't unusual to hear her pray for me. She shared what God was teaching her, and she allowed us to get into some great spiritual discussions. Through that, she inspired much of my own spiritual growth.

I'll never forget the Saturday morning—I was still in bed—that she walked into my room and just stood at the door. I groggily glanced up to see her smiling and to hear her say, "Susie, I'm so proud of you. I know God's hand is on your life in a special way."

Wow! Do you have any idea how much confidence that gave me? It made me feel special. Called. Anointed. Chosen.

Ladies, you can pass on that same kind of powerful spiritual heritage to your own daughters! Do they know you read the Bible? Do they "catch" you doing it?

When was the last time one of your daughters accidentally interrupted you while you were praying?

When moms ask me for help with their daughters, these are the first questions I want them to answer:

- Do you pray for her?
- Does she know you pray for her?
- How do you know she knows you pray for her?

- Does she hear you praying for her?
- Does she see you praying for her?
- Do you pray with her?
- Are you reading and studying God's Word?
- Does your daughter know you read the Bible?
- How do you know she knows you read the Bible?
- Does she hear you reading the Bible?
- Does she see you reading the Bible?
- Do you ever read the Bible together?

I'm not saying that prayer and Bible reading are magic solutions, but many parents who actually read and study the Bible with their children and who pray consistently with their children see the reflection of their own spiritual growth in the lives of their kids.

Does that make sense? Would you consider studying the Bible together as a family? Having devotions together as a family?

MOM AS A SPIRITUAL HERO

On the mother-daughter cruise I mentioned earlier, one of the special speakers we had scheduled was Gracia Burnham. Gracia and her husband, Martin, were missionaries held captive in the Philippine jungles for a little more than a year. Her husband was killed in a rescue attempt, and Gracia now travels and shares her testimony.

I'd heard Gracia speak before, and I'd read her books. I couldn't wait for the moms and daughters on our cruise to hear her story. I shared my enthusiasm with my staff before the cruise. "We don't have a lot of female Christian heroes," I said. "I think Elisabeth Elliot is one, and Amy Carmichael, and Mother Teresa. But who are our spiritual female role models today? I count Gracia Burnham as one of our spiritual heroes, and I want us to pray that our teen girls will see her as a role model."

There weren't many dry eyes in the audience following Gracia's message. Her humble spirit, her sense of humor, and her desire to give God all the glory shouted volumes to our audience. She sold out of her books and other products on the cruise. People flocked to her.

Mom, do you realize that *you* can be your daughter's spiritual hero? You don't have to have a life-and-death testimony as Gracia does. The fact that you, an ordinary woman, are serving an extraordinary God—day in and day out, with bills to pay, schedules to keep, meals to cook—makes you a hero.

But your daughter needs to *see* it. She needs to see you taking the family concerns to your extraordinary God. When you don't know where the money is going to come from to get the car fixed, she needs to hear you praying about it. When you're proud of her for doing something right, she needs to hear you thanking God for it.

Why? Because that's where most of us live. Right in the midst of everyday up-and-down struggles. Right in the middle of an ordinary life, she needs to see you turning to God for strength, for guidance, for money, for answers.

The apostle John—who wrote the last book of the Bible, Revelation—repeats several times that God is the Alpha and Omega. The Beginning and the End. The A and the Z.

I used to wonder why he kept repeating that over and over. And then I began to think of my own life and what I need to know about this. I think the reason John is so repetitive with this is because he knew most of us wouldn't struggle with the beginning and the end.

You probably don't doubt that God created the world. And you're probably sure of the ending—you know that when you die, you'll join Him in heaven. You know that He is the ultimate conqueror. That Satan will eventually be chained and cast into the lake of fire for eternity. In other words, you know you're on the winning team.

You don't have a problem with the beginning and the end. But that's not where most of us live. We're past the beginning. We haven't reached the end yet, but we know what to expect: victory with Christ forever!

But where we live and breathe and sleep and eat and relate is right here in the very middle of life. And this is where it gets sticky. This is where we find ourselves battling depression, worrying about funding our kids' college expenses, wondering why we didn't get the promotion, overwhelmed about the news from the doctor.

And it's as if John wants to remind us that God is not only the Beginning and the End, the A and Z, but He makes up the entire alphabet. He's A and Z and L-M-N-O-P! He's right here with us smack in the middle of our everyday, ordinary, sleeping/waking lives, and He's here to provide everything we need.

Knowing this, why *wouldn't* we want to revel in that strength? Why *wouldn't* we want to read and study His Word? And why *wouldn't* we want to bring our daughters into it with us?

THE BENEFITS ARE GREAT!

Seventeen-year-old Melissa says, "My mom is my spiritual hero. She helps me pray about all kinds of stuff. I'm never embarrassed to pray with her. She makes it really comfortable. We can pray about anything."

Suzanne and her eleven-year-old daughter, Amber, are studying the Bible with Amber's friends. She asked me for a book to get her started. "As soon as the girls and I finish this study," she said, "I'm bringing in all the moms at the end, and we're doing a special mom/daughter nail night. Then I'm hoping to hook the moms into helping me with the next study I want to do."

Even though Amber is only eleven, her mom is wise enough to know that her daughter needs a strong spiritual grounding before entering the teen years. "I think it makes Amber feel special," Suzanne says, "to have her girlfriends over to the house and to know her mom is in charge of leading something fun."

My friend Beth started a group for her daughter and a bunch of inner-city girls. "I'm not sharing the Bible with them yet," she says. "I first have to get to the point where they can all be in the same room without beating each other up. But we're doing self-esteem stuff, and I'm teaching them how special they are in God's eyes. We're taking it slow, but we're making incredible progress!"

Studying God's Word won't look the same for everyone. You may want to get a family Bible from your local Christian bookstore and read one short excerpt at the breakfast or dinner table each day. At the end of each excerpt, discussion questions and a prayer are usually provided. This is a great way to involve the entire family in God's Word.

If your daughter hasn't yet reached her teen years, you may want to purchase a fun children's Bible for her. These are great for helping God's Word come to life for younger kids. They're filled with questions to answer and verses to memorize. The two of you may want to memorize the verses together and answer the questions.

Or you may want to select a devotional guide that will provide a fictional scenario to begin with and a prayer to conclude. If you're wanting more of an actual study on a specific book of the Bible, you can purchase a Bible study book written just for teens. As mentioned earlier, I've written several that can be purchased from my Web site, *www.CloserMomsandDaughters.com.*

There are a multitude of ways you can grow spiritually together. Take a trip to your local Christian bookstore and shop with your daughter for something the two of you are interested in pursuing.

The benefits?

- Your daughter will grow closer to Christ through the reading and studying of His Word.
- Your own relationship with Christ will also deepen.

- As your daughter deepens her intimacy with Christ, she'll also become more confident.
- Your daughter will learn how to articulate her faith and why she believes what she believes.
- As you both grow excited about what you're learning, that excitement will spread to your daughter's friends.
- As she sees and hears you praying and turning to God for everything, she learns there's nothing too big or too small to pray about.
- You and your daughter will grow closer to each other.
- You'll have the opportunity to become your daughter's spiritual hero.

1 JOHN

A Mother-Daughter Bible Study

If you haven't gotten the message yet, I challenge you and your daughter to study God's Word together. And I'm providing an easy start. The rest of this book is dedicated to a mother-daughter Bible study on the book of 1 John. I wrote it just for you. It's a short book (only five chapters), and I've spaced it out in small chunks. If you're able to commit to it every day, it will take twenty-eight days to complete (roughly one month).

Don't feel pressured, however, to space it out this way. Your schedules may not allow you to both study together each day for a month. You may need to shoot for every other day or just two days a week. The issue isn't how quickly you can move through it; the challenge is simply to do it together.

You may even decide to meet together once a week for the study. Again, the time it takes to complete isn't the issue; the focus is on completion.

How do you do it? You can actually read everything together and fill in your answers together. Or you can each do it separately and come together and discuss the questions and your answers after you've completed each section. There are some questions for moms to answer (look for the high-heeled shoe), some questions for daughters to answer (the flip-flop), and some questions for both of you to answer (in bold with no high heel or flip-flop beside it).

You may even want to do this study as a small group by inviting other moms and their teen daughters to join you. You can meet once a week to review the section you've completed.

There's no right or wrong way to do this. Just have fun doing it together. Allow the Lord to continue to draw you closer to each other and closer to Him through His precious Word.

FIRST THINGS FIRST

Erica squirmed in her seat as her youth pastor continued the devotional thought with the youth group. She liked Pastor Kevin. He was young—a surfer dude who was passionate about God. Her friend Rachel sat next to her and elbowed her when Scott walked in late and took a seat toward the back.

"So fine," she mouthed.

"So mine," Erica shot back.

Both girls giggled as Pastor Kevin continued. Erica tried to concentrate on what he was saying, but her mind kept wandering to the group history project that was due in less than a week. *If only I hadn't gotten stuck in a group with Grady*, she thought. *He's so lame. He's not contributing anything, and it's gonna make the rest of us look bad.*

Rachel leaned in and whispered, "Wanna grab a pizza afterward?"

Erica smiled and nodded and again tried to zero in on Pastor Kevin's message. She caught something about joy, but her mind began wandering again. *I hate my life*, she thought. *These past few weeks have been miserable. I really need a new pair of jeans for the fall Harvest Festival, and I still can't believe Mom won't cough up the money. It's not like I'm always asking for stuff. My life reeks.*

"The basis for joy," Pastor Kevin said, "is found in an intimate, growing relationship with Jesus Christ."

Joy. Erica couldn't even remember the last time she experienced true joy. It had been really tough trying to make friends at her new school. That's one reason the history project was so important to her. *If I can't have friends, at least I can do well in history*, she thought. *That is, unless Grady ruins it for everyone.*

Rachel was texting someone on her cell phone, and Erica couldn't help but smile. *At least I have Rachel. Thank goodness for my friends in youth group. Sure wish we went to the same school!*

"Jesus wants to be Lord of your life," Pastor Kevin continued. "And when He's absolutely Lord, you naturally want to serve others."

Erica knew that what he was saying was right. She just couldn't make sense of it in her own life. *I'm not sure I even have time to make Jesus Lord of my life*, she thought. *It's all I can do to make it through even one day at a time at my lame school with no friends.*

"If you're not experiencing true joy," Pastor Kevin said, "there's no reason you can't be."

Erica leaned forward. *What if that's really true?* she thought. *My life would be totally different if I had real joy.*

Her mind continued to wander, and before she knew it, Pastor Kevin was passing a basket around. "I want everyone to take one of these laminated cards," he said. "Put it somewhere where you'll see it often—inside your locker, on your dashboard, on your mirror at home. And each time you look at it, you'll be reminded of the true recipe for genuine joy."

Erica reached inside the basket and pulled out a neon green card that read:

JOY = **J**esus First, **O**thers Second, **Y**ourself Last

Hmmm. I've never thought of it that way before. As students stood and filed out of the youth room, Pastor Kevin stood at the door, making contact with each one as he left. Erica had always admired his passion for people—especially teens.

"Good to see you, Erica," he said. "Rachel, there's a special two-for-one pizza deal at Louie's," he said with a chuckle.

"Hey! How'd you know I was thinking about pizza?"

"I'm a great lip-reader," he teased. "Hey, I want you two to think about something."

"What's that?" Erica said.

"We're starting a special Bible study with the girls in the youth group and their moms."

"At the same time?" Rachel asked.

Pastor Kevin laughed. "Yep. Moms and daughters together."

"What's it about?" Erica said.

"Well, it's kind of a takeoff on what we did tonight."

"You mean something about joy?" Erica said.

Pastor Kevin nodded his affirmation. "We're going to study the book of First John."

"I thought you said it was about joy," Rachel said.

"It is," Pastor Kevin said. "This short little book that the apostle John wrote is called an epistle, and he knew the true equation of real joy."

"Key word being *short*?" Erica asked. "Cuz I have a ton of homework from this lame new school I go to."

Pastor Kevin laughed. "I understand. It's only five chapters long. We're encouraging moms and daughters to do it on a daily basis. If you do, it'll take only twenty-eight days to complete the entire study."

"Wow! That's not even a month," Rachel said.

"I could get into that," Erica said. "And I think my mom would enjoy it too. She's always trying to think of stuff we can do together."

"Great," Pastor Kevin said. "We'll get you started soon."

"*Now* can we get some pizza?" Rachel asked.

"Two for one at Louie's, remember?" Erica said. "We can order two individual-sized; that way I won't have to put up with scraping your mushrooms off of my slices."

THE FACTS OF 1 JOHN

Where is it? In the New Testament. After 2 Peter and right before 2 John.

Who wrote it? The apostle John—known as the "disciple whom Jesus loved." Jesus was close to His twelve disciples. He called them His friends. He mentored them, challenged them, and even rebuked them when they got off course. But He never stopped loving them.

Out of the twelve disciples, however, there were three who were even closer to their Lord: Peter, James, and John. And out of these three, there was one who was extremely close: the apostle John.

Though he grew intimately close with His Lord, he had a rough start. He and his brother, James, had a reputation. They were known as "the sons of thunder." In other words, they were brash, and their tempers flared often. They were probably loud and obnoxious. But Jesus changed their lives. The angry fishermen were transformed into tender apostles. John became known as the disciple of love. Christ makes a big difference when we allow Him to take complete control!

Why should you be interested? John was about one hundred years old when he penned this letter. He was the last living apostle Jesus had personally handpicked. He'd heard and seen a lot in his lifetime. He had allowed Christ to transform him from a flaming hothead into an apostle of love.

God wants to make some changes in *your* life too. He wants to take your weaknesses and turn them into positive avenues for building His kingdom. Do you have a problem with anger? Does your temper often flare? Think no one really understands the fire that burns inside you?

Jump inside the words of someone who's been there. John knew. John understood. And John pointed to Christ as the answer. John was a man who experienced genuine joy in the midst of persecution.

One more thing: Ever wonder if you're really saved? Do spiritual doubts sometimes drive you nuts? As you dive into 1 John, you'll learn how to replace the doubts with faith. You'll trade your questions for solid answers. Who could ask for more?

1 JOHN 1: YOU CAN TRUST HIM!

Day 1

> That which was from the beginning, which we have heard, which we have seen with our eyes, which we have looked at and our hands have touched—this we proclaim concerning the Word of life. (1:1)

✐ **What similarities do you find in the above passage and in the first verse, first chapter of the gospel of John?**

John states that he had seen Christ with his own eyes. The most powerful witness available in any court of law is an eyewitness. John is sharing his credentials as an eyewitness of the Son of God.

> The life appeared; we have seen it and testify to it, and we proclaim to you the eternal life, which was with the Father and has appeared to us. (1:2)

Again, John proves his worth as an eyewitness. He knows what he's writing about because he personally saw Christ, touched Him, and followed Him for three years.

Grab your Bible and turn to Luke 1:2. **What does this verse have to say about an eyewitness?**

Now read 2 Peter 1:16. **What does this Scripture have to say about the value of an eyewitness?**

✎ **Describe a situation in which you were an eyewitness.** (A car accident, history-in-the-making, someone doing something heroic or honorable, etc.)

✎ **How does the fact that you served as an eyewitness to the above add more credibility to your situation than if you were simply relaying the incident secondhand to someone?**

Who is the Word that gives life?

Discuss and Pray

Do you have the life that's available through Christ? If so, is it obvious to those around you? How? (Give specific examples of how others can see Christ living through you.)

If you do have Christ within you and are following Him, you'll want to share Him with others. Pray for each other and ask God to bring each of you an opportunity today to share your faith with someone.

Day 2

Go back two pages and read verse one again. How lucky are we to have this eyewitness account?! Think about it: We get to read the personal account of people who actually walked and talked with the Son of God. We get a firsthand account of what came from heaven through people who saw Christ with their own eyes.

How does this validate Scripture for you?

Now read verse two again. One of the exciting things about Christianity is that it's eternal. Your relationship with Jesus doesn't expire like a library book or a membership to a book club.

Have you ever thought seriously about eternity? About what it will be like to truly live forever? **What are you most looking forward to in eternal life with Christ?**

We proclaim to you what we have seen and heard, so that you also may have fellowship with us. And our fellowship is with the Father and with his Son, Jesus Christ. (1:3)

John's not keeping his knowledge of Christ a secret! He's anxious to share it with others so they too can have a personal relationship with the Lord.

On a scale of 1 to 10 (1 being poor and 10 being great), rank your excitement in sharing your knowledge of Christ with other students:

1 2 3 4 5 6 7 8 9 10

Rank your excitement in sharing your knowledge of Christ with your co-workers or friends:

1 2 3 4 5 6 7 8 9 10

Rank your excitement in sharing your knowledge of Christ with those in your family who don't know Him:

1 2 3 4 5 6 7 8 9 10

List two people with whom you can share your faith within the next month.

1.
2.

Discuss and Pray

If you don't have a passion for sharing Christ with others, ask God to help you see that unbelievers will spend eternity separated from His love. Ask God to give you a genuine burden for those who are spiritually lost.

Day 3

We proclaim to you what we have seen and heard, so that you also may have fellowship with us. And our fellowship is with the Father and with his Son, Jesus Christ. (1:3)

With whom do you have regular fellowship?

Why these specific people?

𝑒 **How often do you experience fellowship with Christ?**

We write this to make our joy complete. (1:4)

John began this letter by telling us that he was a firsthand witness to Christ. In other words, he walked with Him, ate with Him, lived with Him for three years. Now he gives us his second reason for writing this letter. **What is it?**

✴ **Describe the most joyful time in your life thus far.**

✴ **Do you experience true joy in the Lord?**

You may be in the midst of a deep trial, but you can still experience joy in the Lord. Describe the difference between joy and giddiness.

Read Philippians 4:4. *What does the apostle Paul encourage us to do?*

The apostle Paul and the apostle John both experienced joy in the Lord through deep suffering. The emperor Nero tried to boil John alive. When John didn't die, Nero banished the apostle to the rocky, barren island of Patmos. (This is where John wrote the last book of the Bible—Revelation.)

John isn't telling us to do something he himself hasn't mastered. He tells us we can find true joy in a relationship with Christ, and he knows because he has experienced that joy in the midst of many trials.

Describe a time you were able to remain joyful in the Lord even though you were going through a rough time.

Read Psalm 66:1 together. **What are we told to do?**

Now read Psalm 16:11 together. **In what environment are we filled with joy?**

Check out Psalm 43:4. *✐* **How does this verse describe the ultimate source of our joy?**

Discuss and Pray

Use the space provided to write an exclamation of joy to your heavenly Father.

Day 4

This is the message we have heard from him and declare to you: God is light; in him there is no darkness at all. (1:5)

Light is a wonderful attribute of God. *✐* **What are some other characteristics of God?**

Because God is light, and there is no darkness in Him at all, there's nothing we can keep hidden from His knowledge. When we come into His presence, we can't keep anything hidden in the darkness. His light reveals all.

Read Hebrews 4:13. **Though this Scripture doesn't literally mention God's light, how does it allude to God as being light?**

If we claim to have fellowship with him yet walk in the darkness, we lie and do not live by the truth. (1:6)

A lot of people around the world claim to be Christian. **What does it mean, however, when their "talk" doesn't match their "walk"?**

According to 1 John 1:6, if we have a genuine relationship with Christ, what will we no longer do?

Are there some "dark" areas in your life—areas you continue to hold on to instead of surrendering to Christ's authority? What are these areas?

What would need to happen for you to totally surrender these areas of "darkness" to the lordship of Jesus Christ?

But if we walk in the light, as he is in the light, we have fellowship with one another, and the blood of Jesus, his Son, purifies us from all sin. (1:7)

How are you demonstrating living "in the light" of Christ?

One of the outflows of having a relationship with Christ is having fellowship with other believers. If we're genuinely living in His light, we won't lie, gossip, cheat, or make fun of others.

How does your fellowship with other Christians enhance your relationship with Christ?

Discuss and Pray

Right now, ask God to forgive you for holding on to any "dark" areas in your life and give them to Him. Tell Him He has complete authority over every area of your life.

Day 5

But if we walk in the light, as he is in the light, we have fellowship with one another, and the blood of Jesus, his Son, purifies us from all sin. (1:7)

How many sins does Christ's blood cleanse us from?

Imagine you're geocaching in the early evening hours. As you dig for the reward that's buried in the ground, your left hand gets especially dirty. You don't notice it, though, because you're excited about finding the prize and because it's getting dark.

Once you get home, you turn on the lights and see the dirt on your hand. Do you leave it there or wash it off? Hopefully, you'll wash your hands.

As a Christian, you're not exempt from sin. You have power over sin because of Christ within you, but you're still human, and you may struggle with a specific sin. When God shines His light on this specific area of your life, you have a choice: Ignore it and leave the "dirt" there or confess it to Him and allow Him to cleanse it.

And God's cleansing doesn't run out. He doesn't cleanse you today and leave you with the consequences of living with dirt tomorrow. He is all-powerful. His blood will continually cleanse you if you repent with a genuine heart.

If you're wondering if there's unconfessed sin in your life, ask your heavenly Father. Check this out:

> Search me, O God, and know my heart; test me and know my anxious thoughts. See if there is any offensive way in me, and lead me in the way everlasting. (Psalm 139:23–24)

What six things does the psalmist (King David) ask God to do in the above Scripture?

1.

2.

3.

4.

5.

6.

If you ask God to shed light on anything in your life that's not right with Him, He is faithful. He'll do that. But when He does, it's your responsibility to commit that area to Him.

> If we claim to be without sin, we deceive ourselves and the truth is not in us. (1:8)

Turn to Romans 3:23. ✐ **According to this verse, who has sinned?**

Many people today claim that there are no absolutes; there's no true right and wrong. But John tells us that anyone who says he's not a sinner is deceived. The wool has been pulled over his eyes. There are absolutes. There is a right and wrong. Remember, an eyewitness of the Messiah himself is telling us this.

Discuss and Pray

Do you sometimes doubt the absolutes of right and wrong? Ask God to help you live according to His commands.

Day 6

> If we confess our sins, he is faithful and just and will forgive us our sins and purify us from all unrighteousness. (1:9)

What has God promised to do if we confess our sins?

What does it mean to "confess"?

Why can we trust God to do what is right? (Circle all that apply.)

He's without fault.

He is holy.

Just because.

He doesn't care.

He wants us to live in fellowship with Him.

God changes His mind all the time.

We can never fully trust God.

He is truthful.

God never lies.

He loves us.

He is righteous.

God is confusing.

↗ Describe how you felt when you realized you were truly for-given—that God wiped out all record of your sins.

If we confess our sins, he is faithful and just and will forgive us our sins and purify us from all unrighteousness. (1:9)

From what will God cleanse us?

This Scripture doesn't mean that Christ just gives us a spiritual bubble bath. He doesn't just wipe the dirt off of us. He brings restoration. He makes us brand-new!

God is not into sin management. He's not going to organize your sins and line them up neatly in a row. He wants to forgive and remove and restore and totally cleanse. **What's the difference between tidying up and a total cleansing?**

If we claim we have not sinned, we make him out to be a liar and his word has no place in our lives. (1:10)

The Bible tells us in Romans 3:23 that all of us are sinners. The entire human race has sinned. If we deny this fact, we deny the truth of the Bible, and we deny what God has stated as fact.

Describe the difference that God has made in your life now that you're a Christian.

Do those around you see this difference? Can they clearly tell that you once lived in sin but now have true fellowship with the Creator of the universe? How can they tell?

Discuss and Pray

Spend some time thanking God for His willingness to forgive our sins and for His power and desire to continue to cleanse us.

1 JOHN 2: HOW TO KNOW YOU'RE A CHRISTIAN

Day 7

My dear children, I write this to you so that you will not sin. (2:1a)

John, at almost one hundred years of age, considers himself the spiritual father to those he was writing. This endearment also highlights his tenderness and love.

According to this Scripture, why is he writing this letter?

It's obvious that God doesn't want us to sin. He hates sin, and He died for our sins. And He doesn't want us to consciously continue choosing sin over righteousness.

Scripture tells us we can choose to live in a way pleasing to God. We can—through the empowerment of the Holy Spirit—make good choices and live above sin. In other words, we no longer have to be slaves to sin. We can choose to say no to temptation, and through the power of the Holy Spirit saturating our lives, we can choose to do God's will instead of deliberately sinning.

What is sin? Sin isn't simply making a mistake. Sin is an action that goes against the will of God. For example, if God says, "Don't go there," and you go anyway, you've sinned.

If God says, "I want you to do this," and you don't do it, you've gone against His will; you've sinned. There's a difference between sin and mistakes. **Take a moment and identify the difference.**

Sin isn't the same thing as temptation. Grab your Bible and flip to James 1:12. 👠 **What promise is given for those who don't give in to temptation?**

Read James 1:13–16. 👠 **How is temptation defined in this passage?**

Who is the one behind temptation?

It's not a sin to be tempted. Everyone is tempted. Temptation becomes sin only when we yield to it. You can't control who rings your doorbell, but you can control who you invite inside.

You can't control fleeting thoughts and temptations. But when a tempting thought creeps inside your mind, you have the ability to choose whether to let it stay inside, play around with it, and fantasize over it, or to begin praying and walk away from the thought.

John is reminding us that when we have given our lives to Christ (we have confessed our sins, placed our faith in Him, and begun a relationship with Him), we'll still be tempted. But there will come a point in our relationship with Christ (as we're growing closer to Him and deepening our spiritual roots) when we'll realize we can't be all that He commands us to be in our own strength.

And what does He command of us? (Read 1 Peter 1:15–16 for the answer.)

To live a godly lifestyle requires more than a desire to do so; it requires a supernatural power—the power of the Holy Spirit. When we yield 100 percent to His authority, and His power is released within us, we can choose to live in that power and lean on that power when tempted.

John reminds us that with the Holy Spirit empowering us, it is possible to no longer live as a slave to sin. **Is this news to you? Or have you felt you were always doomed to sin?**

Let's check out what the apostle says next:

But if anybody does sin, we have one who speaks to the Father in our defense—Jesus Christ, the Righteous One. (2:1b)

Notice John isn't telling us that we'll never sin anymore. Again, through total submission to the Holy Spirit's power and authority, we can say no to temptation!

But read that verse again. Though we don't have to sin, we're still human. **When we do sin, to whom does John tell us to go?**

And when we seek forgiveness from our heavenly Father, what will happen?

A. He'll forgive us a few more times.

B. He'll always forgive a genuinely repentant heart.

C. He may ignore us, because He's tired of our prayers.

D. His forgiveness might expire.

Never forget that God will always forgive a genuinely repentant heart!

Discuss and Pray

If you've asked Christ into your heart and have accepted His forgiveness for your sins but still haven't given Him absolute, total control, you can do that right now. Here's a prayer to begin with:

Dear Jesus:

Thank you for forgiving my sins and coming into my heart. I'm so grateful that I have a relationship with you. But I don't want to settle for casual Christianity. I want holy intimacy with you.

I surrender *all*.

I yield to your authority, your plans, your will.

Sanctify me and release the power of your Holy Spirit within me. When I'm tempted, help me to call on that supernatural power to say no and to turn in the opposite direction.

In your name I pray.

Amen.

Day 8

He is the atoning sacrifice for our sins, and not only for ours but also for the sins of the whole world. (2:2)

What does it mean to be an "atoning sacrifice"?

Christ doesn't do anything halfway. He not only forgives us, He completely removes the sin from our life!

We know that we have come to know him if we obey his commands. (2:3)

Ever wonder if you're loving God the way He wants you to? This verse tells you how to know that. 🖊 **What's the key?**

What does John 14:15 say we'll do if we really love God?

Rate your obedience factor with the Lord.

1   2   3   4   5   6   7   8   9   10

What would need to happen to help you obey God in every area of your life?

The man who says, "I know him," but does not do what he commands is a liar, and the truth is not in him. (2:4)

John doesn't beat around the bush here, does he? He's extremely straightforward! Have you ever heard a rock star receive a Grammy Award on television and thank God in his acceptance speech? Perhaps you've seen footage of his lifestyle and heard him brag about the sinful life he leads. **According to this Scripture, is he telling the truth?**

But wait a minute! you may be thinking. *As Christians, we're not to judge!*

Yes and no.

We're not to judge for condemnation. Only God has that authority. Check out Matthew 7:1. **What are we told not to do?**

We are not to judge for condemnation. But check out Matthew 7:15–17. **How are we to discern a fruit tree?**

The first part of Matthew 7 tells us not to judge for condemnation, but we're later instructed how to judge for discernment. **Explain the difference.**

But if anyone obeys his word, God's love is truly made complete in him. This is how we know we are in him: Whoever claims to live in him must walk as Jesus did. (2:5–6)

Again, how do we prove our love for God?

How did Jesus live? (Circle all that apply.)

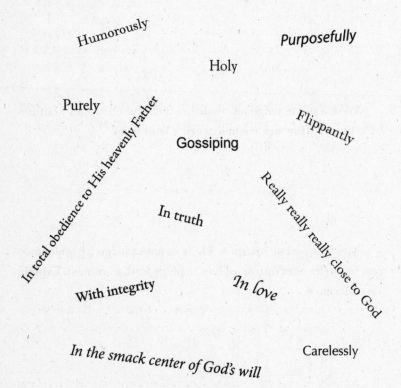

Humorously

Purposefully

Holy

Purely

In total obedience to His heavenly Father

Gossiping

Flippantly

In truth

Really really really close to God

With integrity

In love

In the smack center of God's will

Carelessly

Discuss and Pray

Is there a specific area of your life in which you hesitate to live as Jesus lived? If so, confess that area to God and ask Him to help you live as His Son did.

Day 9

Dear friends, I am not writing you a new command but an old one, which you have had since the beginning. This old command is the message you have heard. (2:7)

John assures us that he's not merely making stuff up. He's teaching what Christ taught. Check out John 13:34–35. *⊘* **How will others know we're Christ's disciples?**

Yet I am writing you a new command; its truth is seen in him and you, because the darkness is passing and the true light is already shining. (2:8)

As we grow closer to Christ—as our relationship with Him deepens and solidifies—the darkness of who and what we were before passes away and we receive more light and knowledge from Him. As we receive more light, we are to live within that light.

> Anyone who claims to be in the light but hates his brother is still in the darkness. (2:9)

Again, John doesn't mince words. 🖋 **Why is it impossible for you to hate another person and truly love God?**

There will always be people who are difficult to get along with and people with whom we choose not to fellowship. But that's different from hatred. Hatred for another person will block your relationship with Christ.

> Whoever loves his brother lives in the light, and there is nothing in him to make him stumble. (2:10)

Read John 8:12. 🖋 **Who is the Light of the World?**

If we truly love God and also love our brothers and sisters, we won't want them to stumble. We won't try to tempt them. And we won't be happy when they encounter difficulties.

🡒 Has there been a time when another Christian has tempted you or caused you to stumble?

That person was not living in the center of God's will. 🡒 John clearly says that we won't cause others to stumble if we're living how?

But whoever hates his brother is in the darkness and walks around in the darkness; he does not know where he is going, because the darkness has blinded him. (2:11)

Bottom line: If you can honestly say that you love others, you're living in the light. If you don't love others, you're living in darkness.

Are you living in the light? Or are you living in the darkness?

Discuss and Pray

Ask God to bring to your mind anyone toward whom you're harboring hatred. Seek His forgiveness and ask Him to help you live in the light and truly love that person as He does.

Day 10

> I write to you, dear children, because your sins have been forgiven on account of his name. (2:12)

John isn't writing only to children; he's addressing Christians of all ages. But this time he doesn't use the word *children* as a term of endearment. He's describing the spiritual state of growth of many people. Many Christians know they're children of God, but they don't take responsibility to learn more. They never "grow up" or mature in their faith.

✐ **What's one commonality among all Christians?**

A. We walk alike.

B. We share an acquired taste in music.

C. We grow spiritually at the same pace.

D. We've all accepted Christ's forgiveness.

> I write to you, fathers, because you have known him who is from the beginning. I write to you, young men, because you have overcome the evil one. I write to you, dear children, because you have known the Father. (2:13)

In 1 John 2:12, he addresses his readers as children. Now he focuses his attention on parents—meaning those who have had a relationship with Christ for a long time. God doesn't want you to stay in the baby stage of Christianity; He wants you to grow spiritually stronger each day you walk with Him.

Read 1 Corinthians 3:2–3. **What does this passage have to say about spiritual growth?**

What helps you maintain consistent spiritual growth?

What hinders you from spiritual growth?

It's impossible to defeat Satan in our own strength. We need the power of the Holy Spirit dwelling within us to overcome. We not only receive strength from the Holy Spirit; John highlights another source of spiritual strength in the next verse.

I write to you, fathers, because you have known him who is from the beginning. I write to you, young men, because you are strong, and the word of God lives in you, and you have overcome the evil one. (2:14)

What lives within the young people to whom John writes?

The Bible is an incredible source of strength for all believers. We're kidding ourselves if we think we can live victorious Christian lives without consistent time in the Word.

Turn to 2 Timothy 3:16. **How do we benefit from the Bible?**

Now read 2 Timothy 3:17. **How does this verse describe the person who studies God's Word?**

Discuss and Pray

How often do you read the Bible? Doing this Bible study is a great start in deepening your relationship with the Lord. But what will happen when this Bible study is finished? Will you make a pledge right now to God that you'll continue your spiritual growth by staying in the Bible?

Day 11

Do not love the world or anything in the world. If anyone loves the world, the love of the Father is not in him. (2:15)

What are "things in the world"?

Check out Romans 12:2. How can we live in the world yet not become part of the world or fall in love with worldly things?

Read 1 John 2:15 again. John shoots straight with his readers. We can't be in love with God and the world, because the world is evil. It's temporarily being run by Satan.

What "worldly things" do you most struggle with not becoming too attached to?

For everything in the world—the cravings of sinful man, the lust of his eyes and the boasting of what he has and does—comes not from the Father but from the world. (2:16)

Read Galatians 5:19–21. 🪐 What similarities do you find in this passage and in 1 John 2:16?

The world and its desires pass away, but the man who does the will of God lives forever. (2:17)

👠 List some of the most beautiful places in the world that you've either seen personally, viewed photos of, or heard about.

As beautiful as those places are, they're only temporary. 👠 What does John say is eternal?

✐ **What does 1 John 2:17 have to say about where your focus should be?**

Discuss and Pray

Ask God to help you discern if you're focused on the right things. Seek His help in making sure your priorities are in line with His will.

Day 12

Dear children, this is the last hour; and as you have heard that the antichrist is coming, even now many antichrists have come. This is how we know it is the last hour. (2:18)

How does John use this verse to express urgency?

If one isn't for Christ, he's actually against Christ. There is no neutral ground spiritually.

They went out from us, but they did not really belong to us. For if they had belonged to us, they would have remained with us; but their going showed that none of them belonged to us. (2:19)

What a sad verse! There were people in the church who "looked the part." They talked about spiritual things and probably took communion with other believers. But eventually what was on the inside came to light on the outside. They weren't true believers.

How can we know if one is a true believer? (Mark all that apply.)

A. He or she will never miss church.

B. He or she will obey God.

C. He or she will love others.

D. He or she will give a lot in church offerings.

E. He or she will demonstrate love for God through a lifestyle dedicated to Jesus.

If we're truly in love with Christ, we'll want to be with other Christians. We'll want to get involved in ministry and support a local church. **Describe your involvement in the local church you attend.**

Why is it important for Christians to be in church and to be involved in a ministry?

But you have an anointing from the Holy One, and all of you know the truth. (2:20)

You have been anointed by the Holy Spirit. God has a high calling on your life. He wants you to stand above the crowd and go against the culture. **List some ways you're currently doing this.**

Discuss and Pray

Thank God for His anointing. Ask Him to continue to reveal His truth to you through His Holy Spirit.

Day 13

I do not write to you because you do not know the truth, but because you do know it and because no lie comes from the truth. (2:21)

John isn't telling his readers anything new. But as he writes, he wants to encourage them in the faith, and he also wants to warn them of the false teaching that was prevalent in their time.

We too are surrounded by false teachings. **List some of the false messages you've heard from other religions.**

Who is the liar? It is the man who denies that Jesus is the Christ. Such a man is the antichrist—he denies the Father and the Son. (2:22)

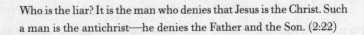 **Who's behind all lies?**

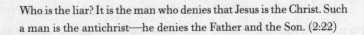 **Who tempts people?**

 Who is trying desperately to keep people from accepting Christ as their Savior?

All lies are summed up in Satan. There are many people who are against Christ. **List some people who have made worldwide headlines who are (or used to be when they were alive) against Christ.**

Anyone who doesn't believe in the Trinity (Father, Son, and Holy Spirit) can't truly call himself a Christian. Many religions believe in a god, but they don't accept that Christ is actually the Son of God. **Why is this an essential belief in Christianity?**

No one who denies the Son has the Father; whoever acknowledges the Son has the Father also. (2:23)

We can't just accept Jesus and choose to stay away from God. Nor can we have the Holy Spirit and not have Christ. Though the Trinity consists of three persons, they are all God. (Yeah, I know it's hard to get your head around this, but the Bible plainly teaches it.) When we become a Christian, we don't simply receive one-third of God; we get all of Him. We get God the Father, Jesus His Son, and the Holy Spirit.

What does it mean to "acknowledge the Son"?

See that what you have heard from the beginning remains in you. If it does, you also will remain in the Son and in the Father. (2:24)

The beginning of what? The beginning is the original Gospel message. To live for God today is to place your faith in One who walked the earth more than two thousand years ago. Christ is consistent! Our faith should also remain consistent. James 1:17 tells us that Jesus doesn't change. He doesn't even shift like a shadow. He remains constant. Therefore, His teachings also remain constant.

What He taught on earth is still relevant today. What you read in the Bible is just as valid now as it was the day each book was penned. **How can you remain rooted in the truth of God that was taught from the beginning of your spiritual journey?**

Discuss and Pray

Tell the Lord your desire to remain strong in Him and to consistently abide in His teachings.

Day 14

And this is what he promised us—even eternal life. (2:25)

How long is eternal life?

> I am writing these things to you about those who are trying to lead you astray. (2:26)

John loves his readers. He's desperately trying to warn them! He wants them to wake up, watch out, and stand guard against the false teachers.

Satan works through non-Christians and mistaken Christians in an attempt to lead believers away from God. **What are some of the strategies he uses? (Mark all that apply.)**

A. Deceit

B. Confusion

C. Bible studies

D. Accountability

E. Lying

F. Teaching false doctrine to Christians

How can you be aware of these false teachers?

One way to be discerning regarding false teaching is to really know the Bible. The more you read it, memorize parts of it, and study it, the better you're able to discern false teaching from what God's Word actually says.

> As for you, the anointing you received from him remains in you, and you do not need anyone to teach you. But as his anointing teaches you about all things and as that anointing is real, not counterfeit—just as it has taught you, remain in him. (2:27)

If you listen to the Holy Spirit within you, He'll provide the discernment you need to distinguish between truth and lies. The Holy Spirit is truth, and He wants you to live in God's truth.

And now, dear children, continue in him, so that when he appears we may be confident and unashamed before him at his coming. (2:28)

Read John 14:15–16. **Besides helping us live in truth, what other things does the Holy Spirit do?**

If you know that he is righteous, you know that everyone who does what is right has been born of him. (2:29)

Children often imitate their parents' behavior and gestures. **Do you find yourself doing something just like your dad or mom would do?** (Maybe it's the way you sneeze, the way you laugh, the way you walk, etc.)

Personality-wise, do you resemble your mom or your dad? In what ways?

God is not only the Father of Jesus Christ; He's also our Father. If we love Him, we'll begin to look like Him in our actions and reactions. Our lifestyle will reflect His personality and love.

Discuss and Pray

Ask the Lord to help you view His Holy Spirit within you as truth, discernment, comfort, help, and guidance. The Holy Spirit will also bring to your mind Scripture verses you've memorized when you need to recall them! He is faithful!

1 JOHN 3: OBEDIENCE = CONFIDENCE

Day 15

> How great is the love the Father has lavished on us, that we should be called children of God! And that is what we are! The reason the world does not know us is that it did not know him. (3:1)

The heavenly Father loves you! The Creator of the universe is crazy about you! 🖊 **How does that make you feel?**

You are God's child. In fact, He loves you just as much as He loves His Son, Jesus. WOW! That's a lot of love. 🖊 **Do you live, act, and react as though you're loved this much by Someone so important?**

> Dear friends, now we are children of God, and what we will be has not yet been made known. But we know that when he appears, we shall be like him, for we shall see him as he is. (3:2)

If you've given your life to Christ, you don't have to hope to someday become a child of God; you're a child of God right now! We don't always act like daughters of the King, but this verse tells us that when He appears, we shall be like Him! ✒ **List some of Christ's characteristics you're looking forward to obtaining.**

Sometimes the longer you're friends with a person, the easier it is to see her shortcomings. This isn't true in your relationship with Christ. The longer you walk with Him, the more and more you grow to love, honor, adore, and respect Him. He has no shortcomings!

Everyone who has this hope in him purifies himself, just as he is pure. (3:3)

Knowing that Christ will someday return should make you live with a greater degree of purity, expectation, and integrity than someone who doesn't know the Lord.

✒ **If Christ were to return tomorrow, what would you be certain to do today?**

Everyone who sins breaks the law; in fact, sin is lawlessness. (3:4)

In Greek—the language in which the New Testament was originally written—this Scripture is talking about one who deliberately, continually sins. This is different from one who is struggling with sin or someone who fails now and then. **Why is deliberately, continually sinning considered living against God's law?**

> But you know that he appeared so that he might take away our sins. And in him is no sin. (3:5)

➤ **Describe why salvation is considered to be the "Good News."**

One of the reasons Christ left heaven and came to earth is listed in the above Scripture. ✎ **What is it?**

Discuss and Pray

Write a short note in the space provided thanking Christ for leaving the glory and splendor of heaven to enter our world for you.

Day 16

> No one who lives in him keeps on sinning. No one who continues to
> sin has either seen him or known him. (3:6)

God has the power to deliver you from being enslaved to sin. Does
this mean you'll never ever sin the rest of your life? It means you don't
have to give in to temptation. You *can* call on and use the power of the
Holy Spirit within you to say no to sin.

But when you do sin, what should you do? (Reread 1 John 2:1–2
for the answer.)

> Dear children, do not let anyone lead you astray. He who does what
> is right is righteous, just as he is righteous. (3:7)

**How can you prevent someone from leading you the wrong
way?**

**Describe a time when you were led the wrong way. What
consequences did you encounter?**

◢ **Describe a time when you led someone the right way; you helped him or her do the right thing.**

He who does what is sinful is of the devil, because the devil has been sinning from the beginning. The reason the Son of God appeared was to destroy the devil's work. (3:8)

In 1 John 3:5, the apostle gave us one reason Jesus came. *◢* **What was it?**

Now, in 1 John 3:8, the apostle gives us another reason Christ came to earth. *◢* **What is it?**

Discuss and Pray

Tell your heavenly Father that you want others to have no doubt that they clearly see Christ in and through you when they look at your life.

Day 17

No one who is born of God will continue to sin, because God's seed remains in him; he cannot go on sinning, because he has been born of God. (3:9)

✒ **Describe some of the major differences in the lifestyle of a believer and the lifestyle of a non-Christian.**

One who has a genuine, growing relationship with Christ doesn't willingly practice sin. We are given a new nature when we accept Christ as our Savior.

This is how we know who the children of God are and who the children of the devil are: Anyone who does not do what is right is not a child of God; nor is anyone who does not love his brother. (3:10)

The apostle John makes it easy to distinguish a Christian from a non-Christian, doesn't he? It's impossible to love God yet not love other people. There will be those in your life who are difficult to get along with and people you don't enjoy being around. **Describe the difference between loving someone because God loves that person through you and how you act when you truly enjoy someone's company.**

This is the message you heard from the beginning: We should love one another (3:11)

Describe three people in your life who truly make you feel loved and what they do that makes you feel this way.

1.

2.

3.

Do not be like Cain, who belonged to the evil one and murdered his brother. And why did he murder him? Because his own actions were evil and his brother's were righteous. (3:12)

We learn in the book of Hebrews that Cain offered God a sacrifice from his own works, and his brother Abel offered God a sacrifice in faith. God always looks at our heart. He values obedience and faith much more than our works.

God rejected Cain's sacrifice and accepted Abel's. Cain was so filled with jealousy, bitterness, and envy that he killed his brother.

Describe a time when you were so jealous, envious, or bitter that you acted it out. And what were the consequences?

Discuss and Pray

Ask God to bring to light any jealousy, envy, or bitterness in your life. Instead of hanging on to them, seek His forgiveness and commit them to the Lord.

Day 18

Do not be surprised, my brothers, if the world hates you. (3:13)

🖋 **Describe a time people treated you wrong because of your faith.**

Grab your Bible and turn to the gospel of John, verses 15:18–19.
🥿 **What does this passage say about being hated?**

We know that we have passed from death to life, because we love our brothers. Anyone who does not love remains in death. (3:14)

You can know for certain if you're a Christian. John compares having a relationship with Christ as leaving death and coming into life. **How is this an accurate picture of Christianity?**

Anyone who hates his brother is a murderer, and you know that no murderer has eternal life in him. (3:15)

John is building on what he heard Jesus say. Read Matthew 5:21–22. 🦶 **How does this Scripture validate 1 John 3:15?**

Check out Proverbs 18:21. Killing a person doesn't always have to be a "physical death." 👞 **What are other ways we can "kill" a person based on this verse?**

This is how we know what love is: Jesus Christ laid down his life for us. And we ought to lay down our lives for our brothers. (3:16)

Christ is our ultimate example. He embodies the entire meaning of love. He *is* love. How much does God love you? Check out John 3:16 for the answer.

We may not lay down our lives for our brothers and sisters through a physical death, but we can give our lives in other ways. **List some:**

Describe a time when another Christian gave his or her life for you.

Discuss and Pray

Ask God to make you aware of ways you can "give your life away" on a daily basis.

Day 19

If anyone has material possessions and sees his brother in need but has no pity on him, how can the love of God be in him? (3:17)

Again, John leaves no room for guessing. We're either living in God's love and showing it to those around us, or we're not.

Dear children, let us not love with words or tongue but with actions and in truth. (3:18)

You may have heard the phrase "talk is cheap." Anyone can say he loves someone, but to actually put love into action is an entirely different matter. **How did Christ put love into action?**

🥿 **Describe how you've loved two people in the past month by your actions and your concern.**

This then is how we know that we belong to the truth, and how we set our hearts at rest in his presence whenever our hearts condemn us. For God is greater than our hearts, and he knows everything. (3:19–20)

Your relationship with Christ can't be based on feelings; it must be based on fact and faith. We can't always trust our heart—or our feelings. Look up Psalm 26:2. 👠 **According to this Scripture, what should we ask God to do in regard to our heart?**

Now read Psalm 139:23. **Compare this verse with Psalm 26:2.**

Though we can't always trust our feelings, God does use His Holy Spirit to work through our heart and conscience to help us know when we've done wrong. That's why it's so important to consistently ask God to search our heart and to show us if there's anything we need to confess or if there's anything we're doing to displease Him.

> Dear friends, if our hearts do not condemn us, we have confidence before God and receive from him anything we ask, because we obey his commands and do what pleases him. (3:21–22)

✐ **How can we live with a pure heart?** (Check out 1 Timothy 1:5.)

With a pure heart, you can be confident in your relationship with the Lord. *✐* **What does it mean to approach the throne of God with boldness?**

How confident are you in your relationship with Christ?

1   2   3   4   5   6   7   8   9   1 0

Discuss and Pray

Ask the Lord to search your heart and show you anything in your life that's not right with Him. Ask Him to help you be confident in your relationship with Him.

Day 20

We ended day 19 with 1 John 3:21–22, but let's combine those verses with where we're picking up now.

> Dear friends, if our hearts do not condemn us, we have confidence before God and receive from him anything we ask, because we obey his commands and do what pleases him. And this is his command: to believe in the name of his Son, Jesus Christ, and to love one another as he commanded us. (3:21–23)

This doesn't mean that God is a Santa in the sky granting your every wish. But He is committed to meeting the needs of His children.

✐ **Describe the difference between *needs* and *wants*.**

God loves to give good gifts to His children. **List five good things He's given you.**

1.

2.

3.

4.

5.

Again, the apostle emphasizes the necessity of Christians to genuinely love others. ◢ **What else in this Scripture does God command we do?**

Those who obey his commands live in him, and he in them. And this is how we know that he lives in us: We know it by the Spirit he gave us. (3:24)

Read Romans 8:9. ◢ **To whom is the Holy Spirit given?**

God's Holy Spirit within us is kind of like a "brand." You can tell what farmer owns which cows by the brand on their hides. *Describe how the Holy Spirit is God's brand on your life.*

Discuss and Pray

Thank God for His special brand on your life. Ask Him to help you become more sensitive to the Holy Spirit's leading every day.

1 JOHN 4: IT'S ALL ABOUT LOVE

Day 21

> Dear friends, do not believe every spirit, but test the spirits to see whether they are from God, because many false prophets have gone out into the world. (4:1)

Just because someone claims to be a Christian doesn't make him one. John encourages us to be discerning with what we hear. **What does that mean?**

The Bible tells us we will encounter wolves in sheep's clothing. Grab your Bible and turn to Matthew 7:15. **What does this Scripture say about those who deceive?**

Now read Acts 20:29. **What are we warned about in this verse?**

Many people hold a microphone, speak articulately, and say positive things. This doesn't mean they're speaking the Word of God. John tells us to "test the spirits." How do we do that? He gives us instruction in the next Scripture.

This is how you can recognize the Spirit of God: Every spirit that acknowledges that Jesus Christ has come in the flesh is from God, but every spirit that does not acknowledge Jesus is not from God. This is the spirit of the antichrist, which you have heard is coming and even now is already in the world. (4:2–3)

All Christian messengers (preachers, evangelists, missionaries, Sunday school teachers, etc.) should teach not only that Christ was human but that He's also the Son of God. One who denies one or the other isn't a messenger of God.

The Bible is clear that there will be an antichrist, but many people display an "anti-Christ" attitude. They may claim to be Christians, but if their words about Jesus don't match what the Bible says, they are really against Christ.

Read Matthew 24:5. **What does this verse say about those who are anti or against Christ?**

You, dear children, are from God and have overcome them, because the one who is in you is greater than the one who is in the world. (4:4)

As strong as Satan is, who is stronger?

Describe a time when God helped you defeat the devil.

Discuss and Pray

Tell the Lord you want to be discerning. Ask Him to guide you with His wisdom.

Day 22

They are from the world and therefore speak from the viewpoint of the world, and the world listens to them. (4:5)

A cherry tree produces cherries. An apple tree grows apples. A person of the world (one who doesn't have a relationship with Christ) will act like the world and relate to the world.

You are not of this world! Keep your eyes focused on eternity with Christ. When you can't relate to those around you, or when you don't fit in, be glad! You're not supposed to fit in with the world.

Give an example of a time when you didn't fit in with the world.

We are from God, and whoever knows God listens to us; but whoever is not from God does not listen to us. This is how we recognize the Spirit of truth and the spirit of falsehood. (4:6)

Don't be discouraged when the world doesn't want to listen to you talk about the Lord. You can't make someone accept God's teaching; only the Holy Spirit can do that. Continue to share your faith with those around you and trust the Lord to do the rest.

Dear friends, let us love one another, for love comes from God. Everyone who loves has been born of God and knows God. (4:7)

👠 **Why should we love each other?**

👠 **Where does love come from?**

Whoever does not love does not know God, because God is love. (4:8)

Again, John makes it extremely clear how to tell who's a Christian and who's not. As mentioned previously, we are not to judge for condemnation; but we *have* been instructed to carefully discern a person's teachings.

It's easy to love those who love us, but it's often difficult to love those who are hateful toward us. **Describe a situation in which you found it difficult to love in your own strength but you allowed God to love someone through you.**

Discuss and Pray

Thank God for His desire and ability to love anyone and everyone through you.

Day 23

> This is how God showed his love among us: He sent his one and only Son into the world that we might live through him. (4:9)

What are the similarities between the above Scripture and John 3:16?

> This is love: not that we loved God, but that he loved us and sent his Son as an atoning sacrifice for our sins. (4:10)

How does the fact that God gave His Son for us demonstrate His love for us?

Dear friends, since God so loves us, we also ought to love one another. (4:11)

Why should we love others?

No one has ever seen God; but if we love one another, God lives in us and his love is made complete in us. (4:12).

How can people see God in your life through your love for them?

Perhaps you've heard the phrase "You may be the only Bible those around you see." **What does this mean, and how does it relate to the above verse?**

We know that we live in him and he in us, because he has given us of his Spirit. (4:13)

Again, God's Holy Spirit acts as a "brand" or as proof that we belong to the Father. He is our seal that shows the world to whom we belong. **How does this verse provide security for you?**

Discuss and Pray

Thank God for the security He provides through His Spirit. Thank Him for wanting you more than you can articulate.

Day 24

And we have seen and testify that the Father has sent his Son to be the Savior of the world. (4:14)

Again, John shares his credentials as an eyewitness to Christ's life on earth. **How does this make this study more believable and reliable to you?**

If anyone acknowledges that Jesus is the Son of God, God lives in him and he in God. (4:15)

Compare John 5:24 with the above Scripture.

And so we know and rely on the love God has for us. God is love. Whoever lives in love lives in God, and God in him. (4:16)

God is trustworthy, dependable, and faithful. Because He loves us, we'll in turn love others if we truly belong to Him and live in obedience to Him.

In this way, love is made complete among us so that we will have confidence on the day of judgment, because in this world we are like him. (4:17)

When we place our faith in Christ and begin fellowship with Him, He begins making us like Him. 🖋 **According to the above verse, how should this make you feel about Judgment Day?**

There is no fear in love. But perfect love drives out fear, because fear has to do with punishment. The one who fears is not made perfect in love. (4:18)

Why do you not need to fear God's judgment?

How comfortable are you in God's love?

1   2   3   4   5   6   7   8   9   10

We love because he first loved us. (4:19)

When did God begin loving you? (Mark all that apply.)

A. When you were still a sinner

B. When you started attending church

C. When you were born

D. When you placed your faith in Him

E. Before you were even conceived

If anyone says, "I love God," yet hates his brother, he is a liar. For anyone who does not love his brother, whom he has seen, cannot love God, whom he has not seen. (4:20)

According to this Scripture, who are liars?

And he has given us this command: Whoever loves God must also love his brother. (4:21)

Notice that God doesn't *suggest* we love others. Nor does He give us the choice to love others if we want to. He *commands* us to love. **How does this command affect everything in your life?**

Discuss and Pray

Ask God to saturate you with His love. Tell Him you truly want to love others as He does.

1 JOHN 5: KNOWING GOD, KNOWING TRUTH

Day 25

Everyone who believes that Jesus is the Christ is born of God, and everyone who loves the father loves his child as well. (5:1)

How does this reflect what John has already said thus far in this letter? What other Scriptures in 1 John are similar to this verse?

This is how we know that we love the children of God: by loving God and carrying out his commands. (5:2)

How do obedience to God and loving others complement each other?

This is love for God: to obey his commands. And his commands are not burdensome, for everyone born of God overcomes the world. This is the victory that has overcome the world, even our faith. (5:3–4)

This Scripture gives you the secret of remaining spiritually victorious. 👠 **What is it?**

> Who is it that overcomes the world? Only he who believes that Jesus is the Son of God. (5:5)

Christians are winners! And because of God's Holy Spirit inside you, you have the power to defeat Satan. 👠 **How does this make you feel?**

Discuss and Pray

Ask God to continually remind you of the Holy Spirit's power within you that can enable you to defeat the devil when you're tempted.

Day 26

> This is the one who came by water and blood—Jesus Christ. He did not come by water only, but by water and blood. And it is the Spirit who testifies, because the Spirit is the truth. (5:6)

John was not only an eyewitness of Christ's life on earth, he also witnessed the Lord's death. Read John 19:33–35. ✎ **What water does John speak of here?**

Christ not only shed blood for us, He completely died. The water from His side was a physical sign that death had occurred. We know today that it was the clear fluid from the pericardium, the sac that encloses the heart. That means the spear pierced Jesus' heart. **Three days after His death on the cross, what did Christ do?**

For there are three that testify: the Spirit, the water and the blood; and the three are in agreement. (5:7–8)

How can you know that you're a Christian? The Holy Spirit within you bears witness—He's your seal from God. The water from Christ's side proves He was dead (He died for *you*), and His blood cleanses you from all sin.

We accept man's testimony, but God's testimony is greater because it is the testimony of God, which he has given about his Son. (5:9)

Turn to Matthew 3:17. ✎ **What has God said about His Son?**

Anyone who believes in the Son of God has this testimony in his heart. Anyone who does not believe God has made him out to be a liar, because he has not believed the testimony God has given about his Son. And this is the testimony: God has given us eternal life, and this life is in his Son. (5:10–11)

✎ **What can we draw from this passage about Hindus, Buddhists, and any other religion that doesn't profess Christ as God's Son?**

👞 **What are other religions that don't believe Christ is God's Son?**

Discuss and Pray

Ask God to help you share your faith with people who have opposing religious beliefs to Christianity.

Day 27

He who has the Son has life; he who does not have the Son of God does not have life. (5:12)

John, again, doesn't leave us guessing about who's a Christian and who's not. 🖊 **Based on this verse, how can Christians be identified?**

I write these things to you who believe in the name of the Son of God so that you may know that you have eternal life. (5:13)

🖊 **Why is John writing this letter?**

This is the confidence we have in approaching God: that if we ask anything according to his will, he hears us. (5:14)

Our prayers should be according to God's will. If you're truly walking with Christ, you'll want His will in every situation you encounter. God not only *hears* your prayers, He *answers* them. Every time you pray, He answers. He doesn't always answer in the way you want Him to, nor does He always answer immediately. But be assured that God always answers prayer.

Check out this promise from the Old Testament:

But these things I plan won't happen right away. Slowly, steadily, surely, the time approaches when the vision will be fulfilled. If it seems slow, do not despair, for these things will surely come to pass. Just be patient! They will not be overdue a single day! (Habakkuk 2:3 TLB)

God isn't early; but He's never late.

And if we know that he hears us—whatever we ask—we know that we have what we asked of him. (5:15)

When we're praying in line with God's will, we're not praying selfishly. When we say, "These things I pray in Jesus' name," we're really saying, "I'm praying this prayer as I believe Jesus would pray to the Father."

Jesus wouldn't ask for something silly. When He prayed, He was serious about seeking, knowing, and obeying the will of His Father.

Will knowing this make a difference in your prayer life? If so, what kind of difference?

Discuss and Pray

Read the Lord's Prayer out loud for your prayer time today. It's found in Matthew 6:5–13.

Day 28

> If anyone sees his brother commit a sin that does not lead to death, he should pray and God will give him life. I refer to those whose sin does not lead to death. There is a sin that leads to death. I am not saying that he should pray about that. (5:16)

What is the sin that leads to death? (See Matthew 12:31 for the answer.)

Now check out Genesis 6:3. **Copy this verse in the space provided.**

There comes a point in time when God's Spirit will not mesh with man's spirit. When is this time? When man continues to reject, ignore, walk away from, and say no to God, there comes a time he no longer hears or feels the Holy Spirit talking to his heart about the Lord. He's deafened his ears to the voice of God and has shut the door on the Father. Dying in unbelief is the sin that leads to death.

> All wrongdoing is sin, and there is sin that does not lead to death. (5:17)

All of us will die physically, but those who die in unbelief are also dead spiritually.

> We know that anyone born of God does not continue to sin; the one who was born of God keeps him safe, and the evil one cannot harm him. (5:18)

The Christian doesn't try to become a better sinner; he or she strives to become more and more like Christ. **How do you see God specifically working in your life right now?**

First John 5:18 says the Evil One can't touch Christians. What does that mean?

Satan can tempt you but can't control you if the Holy Spirit rules your life. A Christian filled with the Holy Spirit cannot be demon-possessed. 🖊 **Read again 1 John 4:4 and copy it in the space provided.**

> We know that we are children of God, and that the whole world is under the control of the evil one. (5:19)

Satan currently controls the world—but it's only temporary. We know that God is greater. And by reading the book of Revelation, we know that Christ will return to earth as Judge and in complete control. He will defeat Satan forever. **How does this make you feel?**

We know also that the Son of God has come and has given us understanding, so that we may know him who is true. And we are in him who is true—even in his Son Jesus Christ. He is the true God and eternal life. (5:20)

Christianity isn't a religion; it's a lifestyle, a relationship; it's Jesus Christ as Lord. If you have Christ, you have salvation, and you have eternal life.

🖊 **How does 1 John 5:20 banish any doubts you may have regarding your relationship with Christ?**

Dear children, keep yourselves from idols. (5:21)

Anything that stands between you and God is an idol—or a false god. John wasn't alluding to sports stars, movie stars, or rock stars in this verse—they weren't around in his day. But *anyone* or *anything* that stands between you and God is an idol. Lust, covetousness, a friendship, a relationship, your car, sports, etc.

↗ What things or people do you sometimes tend to place too much emphasis on?

Discuss and Pray

Tell God that you not only want Him to be important in your life but that you want Him to be your life. Ask Him to teach you how to revolve your life around Him 24-7.

You did it! You've just completed the fifth and last chapter of 1 John. How have you grown from studying this letter?

Yes, you've completed the book of 1 John, but don't stop here! Strive to read the entire Bible! Do you realize that if you read three chapters every Monday through Saturday and five chapters every Sunday, you'll have automatically read the whole Bible in one year?

This would be a fantastic challenge for moms and daughters to accomplish together.

It'll change your lives!

PRAYER OF SALVATION FOR MOTHERS

Dear Jesus,

I believe you are who you claimed to be: the Messiah, the Son of God, the One who can forgive my sins and give me eternal life.

I also believe you came to earth in human form to die on a cross for my sins. You did that because you knew I could never pay the price. I can't thank you enough for that!

I admit I'm a sinner. I'm so sorry I've broken your commands and have disobeyed you. Will you forgive me? I believe the Bible is your holy Word; I believe it's true. And you promised if I would seek your forgiveness, you would grant it.

Dear Jesus, I'm asking for your forgiveness with a repentant heart. I truly do want to change and follow you the rest of my life.

So I'm placing my faith in you. I believe you have now forgiven my sins, because I asked in humility and genuineness. Thank you! Thank you so much for forgiving me and for loving me more than I can even grasp.

Dear Jesus, come into my heart and guide my life. I want my daughter to know you. I want her to see you in my actions and reactions. Help me to draw my daughter into an intimate relationship with you.

And Jesus, help me to develop intimacy with you. Help me to read the Bible consistently and to turn to you for guidance. Help me to establish a strong prayer life. Teach me to talk with you about everything. Increase my faith. Help me to get involved in church.

Thank you for saving me! Thank you for the gift of eternal life. I realize this is only the beginning. Now help me to actually grow strong and deep in you.

I love you, Jesus. And I want to love you more and more every day of my life. Help me to be the Christian mother to my daughter that she so desperately needs.

I pray these things in your name.

Amen.

More Expert Advice for Moms

Get Inside the Mind of Your Teen Daughter

Just when your teen daughter needs you the most, she may completely shut down around you. She wants to talk to you—she just doesn't know how. Taking you inside her heart and mind, this book helps you see through the silences, showing you what she's going through and how you can be there for her.

What Your Daughter Isn't Telling You
by Susie Shellenberger and Kathy Gowler

DISCARD